THE LONG WAY HOME

THE LONG WAY HOME

*A Testimony of God's Grace
and an Invitation to Come Home*

Brittany N. Gross-Jolly

Published by Graceful Seed® Publishing
A division of Graceful Seed LLC
New Jersey, USA
Rooted in Truth, Growing in Grace.

Copyright © 2026 by Brittany N. Gross-Jolly

All rights reserved. No part of this publication may be reproduced, distributed, or transmitted in any form or by any means, including photocopying, recording, or other electronic or mechanical methods, without the prior written permission of the publisher, except in the case of brief quotations embodied in critical reviews and certain other noncommercial uses permitted by copyright law.

Published by **Graceful Seed® Publishing**, a division of Graceful Seed LLC

Printed in the United States of America

ISBN 979-8-9934703-1-3 (Paperback)
ISBN 979-8-9934703-3-7 (Hardcover)
ISBN 979-8-9934703-2-0 (eBook)

Unless otherwise noted, Scripture quotations are taken from the **Christian Standard Bible® (CSB)**, Copyright © 2017 by Holman Bible Publishers. Used by permission. Christian Standard Bible® and CSB® are federally registered trademarks of Holman Bible Publishers. Portions of commentary or study notes are quoted from The Tony Evans Study Bible, © 2019 by Tony Evans. Used by permission of Holman Bible Publishers. All rights reserved.

Scripture quotations marked (KJV) are from the **King James Version of the Bible,** which is in the public domain.

Scripture quotations marked (NKJV) are from the **New King James Version®**, Copyright © 1982 by Thomas Nelson. Used by permission. All rights reserved.

Scripture quotations marked (NIV) taken from The Holy Bible, **New International Version®, NIV®.** Copyright © 1973, 1978, 1984, 2011 by Biblica, Inc. Used with permission of Zondervan. All rights reserved worldwide. www.zondervan.com

Calder, Helen. *Prophetic Insight: Greatness, Glory and the Faces of Lions.* Enliven Publishing, 2013.https://www.enlivenpublishing.com/2013/07/30/prophetic-insight-the-faces-of-lions/.

"Biblical Meaning of Seeing a Hawk." *Hymns and Verses.* https://hymnsandverses.com/biblical-meaning-of-seeing-a-hawk/.

"Classification of Demons." *Wikipedia.* https://en.wikipedia.org/wiki/Classification_of_demons.

Perry, Sara. *365 Days of Courage.* BroadStreet Publishing Group, February 2023.

Cover design and interior typesetting by Jonathan Lewis

Glory be to the Most High God, my Abba, whose grace sustained me through this journey and made this book possible. To Jesus Christ, our Lord and Savior—the author and finisher of my faith.

To my father and mother, who gave it all they had in raising three children—thank you for providing a moral compass and cultivating a foundation of integrity, security and love. There are no words to express my love or the depth of gratitude I have for your sacrifices.

To my beloved family and friends—may we never forget that love conquers all.

And to my husband, who weathered the storms—
I love you.

Contents

Introduction	1
Foreshadow	3
Religion and Background	7
PART ONE: THE JOURNEY	**11**
When I Lost My Way	12
The Quiet Drift	15
Elemental Immersion: Seeking Power in Nature	20
Ancestralization: Calling on the Ancestors	45
The Gift of Prophecy: Vision and Foresight	67
Black Magic and Tarot	81
Divinations: The Illusion of Clarity	88
Robin and the Power Animal Retrieval	115
Reiki and Crystal Phase	137
My Cry Out to God	151
PART TWO: WHEN THE VEIL WAS LIFTED	**167**
Sprinting Back to God	168
The Call for Deliverance	175
Marriage: Unequal Yoking	187
Trust Him	199
My Wrestle with God	209

PART THREE: GOD'S GRACE — 221

    The Road to Restoration — 222

    Let Your Light Shine — 229

    Trusting God — 233

    The Call Is Not Always Comfortable — 242

    The Season of Building — 249

Epilogue: To the One Still Wandering — 255

Introduction

The Long Way Home is more than a story—it's a journey of return.

Within these pages, you'll find pieces of my path back to God after being led astray by deception, distraction, and the weight of life's battles. But this book isn't only about where I've been; it's an invitation for you to look within your own story and discover where God has been leading you all along.

You'll notice that the book unfolds in two timelines: the past that shaped me and the present that restored me—woven together to reveal how God's hand was never absent, even in seasons of distance. Each chapter offers both narrative and reflection, blending testimony with truth so that my lessons can become landmarks for your own faith journey. Consider this book a companion on your road home—a guide to help you recognize the tricks of the enemy, learn to hear and trust God's voice, confront what has kept you bound, and walk in the freedom of redemption. Welcome to The Long Way Home. May these words lead you closer to the One who never stopped calling your name.

Foreshadow

Religion, throughout history, has shaped empires, inspired movements, and fueled some of the world's most devastating conflicts. Few forces have shaped humanity more profoundly or divided it more bitterly. Religion is one of humanity's greatest sources of division—sparking wars, fueling conflicts, causing suffering, and provoking endless debate.

The day came when I found myself on the other end of the phone doing this very thing with my brother. We disagreed about our walk with God: at the time, he had recently become Catholic, and I considered myself a believer, a child of God Almighty and a spiritual woman.

This argument was devastating on so many levels. He told me, at that time in my life, that I was being spiritually attacked. I responded, "Well yes, I am—I'm being attacked by you. Can't you see? You're attacking my journey with God and my way of expressing how He works in my life." My brother and I had only just begun to recover a relationship I never thought could be broken. And after this call, it felt like everything came crashing back down. I was asking God for answers, this couldn't be the way. In that moment, I saw no light, no love. What was happening?

That call weighed on me; it was hard to sleep that night. By 4 a.m. the next morning, I was already awake. One thing he said echoed in my mind: "You cannot look outside of God and His Word for answers." On that note, I picked up my Bible to read Scripture, deciding I would start my days this way from now on. The book slipped from my hand, out of its cover, and landed open on the floor on 2 Corinthians. What caught my attention was a single sentence, highlighted in red—His words, standing out on the page:

2 Corinthians 12:9 (KJV)
My Grace is sufficient for thee: for my strength is made perfect in weakness.

I sat and received the word. To my surprise the LORD was not finished with me. As I sat in stillness I could hear Savannah, my dog, rumbling in the trash bin. It was so loud and disruptive; it broke my focus. I went over to see what she had, and it was a paper she had removed from the bin. It was directions to a package I had opened the day before, and on it in bold read **"Read and Follow All Safety Instructions."** I took this very literally and in that moment, I had a sense that I should go back and read the entire page, not just what was highlighted in red. What a revelation it was! My jaw dropped as I read on:

2 Corinthians 12:20–21 (KJV)
For I fear, lest, when I come, I shall not find you such as I

would, and that I shall be found unto you such as ye would not: lest there be debates, envyings, wraths, strifes, backbitings, whisperings, swellings, tumults: And lest, when I come again, my God will humble me among you, and that I shall bewail many which have sinned already, and have not repented of the uncleanness and fornication and lasciviousness which they have committed.

2 Corinthians 13:1–2 (KJV)
This is the third time I am coming to you. In the mouth of two or three witnesses shall every word be established. I told you before, and foretell you, as if I were present, the second time; and being absent now I write to them which heretofore have sinned, and to all others, that, if I come again, I will not spare.

When I reached chapter 13 my body froze. I wanted to disappear; I felt in that moment I had gotten it all wrong. Everything I thought was right was just the opposite. Had I been tricked? Did I fall into the 'new age' trap …?

A father scolding his rebel child is how the Scripture read, and this indeed had been the third time God had come to me. I fell to my knees asking for forgiveness—I wept and prayed. I quickly searched for my phone and called my brother and asked for his forgiveness, still weeping and sitting in the seat of God's warning. I could barely get out my words, I cried, and we cried together. This conversation had woken me up from a deep spiritual slumber.

I was broken. I had gone astray and didn't realize I was deceived on so many levels. I did not know what to do or how to proceed from there, what was right or how far I had gone. But I knew I had to get back to God, and I had to run!

> **THE TRUTH I KNOW NOW**
>
> **Hebrews 4:12**
> For the word of God is living and powerful, and sharper than any two-edged sword, penetrating as far as the separation of soul and spirit, joints and marrow. It is able to judge the thoughts and intentions of the heart.

Religion and Background

I come from a Christian upbringing, but we did not go to church. My Dad studied the word avidly: he is a Christian man with a healthy fear of the Lord. He always said, "I have church right here in my heart and in my home." He never pushed any religion on us: we said our grace before eating, prayers at night, and we respected the Lord. I'm the youngest of three, with two older brothers. We grew up close: we weren't perfect, but we had love in our home and took care of one another. In our childhood there was a Jehovah's Witness named Mrs. Pierce that would come by for Bible study during our summer breaks in grade school. She was an elderly lady, but she came faithfully, at the same time every week. My eldest brother was old enough to get out of the study sessions. I can remember hearing all my friends outside playing when it was time for us to have Bible study; this was challenging as a kid, but Dad made sure we attended faithfully and attentively and would even ask for a report of our behavior during the study. What I remember of these times is that I always asked questions: so many and in such depth that Mrs. Pierce would have to write them down and come back with the answers. She always came back with her handwritten answers to my questions. They didn't always answer my questions completely, but she never ignored them. I loved and respected her for that. God rest her soul; she left a lasting impression on many lives.

As I grew older, I attended church with my friends here and there, but I didn't have a solid foundation in the church or an active relationship with God. I really didn't know what it meant to have one. I've always felt his presence and He has shown up for me in times of my youth: this convinced me that God is indeed real and living. One would think that is enough, but life and the enemy have their way of sneaking in and robbing the little you have if your relationship with the LORD is not cultivated, rooted, and maintained throughout your life.

I can recall many bizarre things happening in my life that would suggest opposing forces were at play in our reality. Even with this I ventured out on my journey and took the long way home … every step away from God I took unknowingly felt like freedom—until it didn't. At first, the distance looked like independence, like writing my own story without boundaries or restraint. In so many ways I was living like I was strong enough to carry the weight of my own life, and wise enough to know what was best. But freedom without truth is only another kind of bondage, and I didn't realize how heavy the chains had become until it was almost too late.

What began as a slow drift turned into a long exile, a season where lies felt like truth and truth felt out of reach. It began with small compromises, quiet lies I told myself, and subtle deceptions that wrapped around me like threads. A whisper here, a doubt there, until those threads became cords, and those cords became chains. Entangled. What I thought was a wide-open road was leading me deeper into captivity.

But even in the wilderness, God never lost sight of me. He was there, calling me home. Even when I was too blind to see Him and too stubborn to listen, He was there. Patient. Waiting. His voice didn't thunder through the clouds—it came like a steady pulse, a soft reminder that I was not beyond His reach.

This is the story of how I wandered, how I was deceived, how I stumbled in darkness. But it is also the story of grace—how God met me in the ruins and carried me home. It is my testimony, but it may also be yours. Because no matter how far you feel you have strayed, our Heavenly Father is calling His people home.

PART ONE

The Journey

When I Lost My Way

The year 2020 was rough for everyone, but it felt personal to me. I lost my best friend, and my wedding was canceled two weeks prior to our scheduled departure to our destination venue, which took a strenuous amount of time and emotion to plan. We couldn't agree on a local venue and that resulted in settling on a destination. I remember my (at the time) fiancé and I being glued to the news, watching countries announce the closing of their borders: this too felt very personal. My world, like many others, was shifting. I made the difficult decision to leave a job that no longer fulfilled me, despite not having a signed offer from my next prospective employer—an opportunity that ultimately fell through. Until that moment, I had never been without my own source of income, a trait I had long carried with pride. Independence was not just a preference but a defining principle, one I upheld in every circumstance, always ensuring that I could stand on my own in any situation. It was a core part of my identity. Yet, as I would soon learn, this was only the beginning of my challenges.

I remember looking out my office window one morning in deep thought and reflection and in the near distance I saw an all-white bird, a dove or mourning bird on a tree in the backyard. It was the dead of winter: the trees were bare and it stood out so beautifully—I remember journaling it. I knew that seeing this had a much deeper meaning. I wasn't where I am now in God, so I just took it as a good sign; I didn't recognize it then for what I know now. The likelihood of seeing this bird in normal weather conditions is extremely rare, so seeing it during this time made it that much more impressive. I gazed at it with great wonder, wondering what message it was bearing. The all-white coloration, or albinism, makes these birds a target in their natural habitats; they stand out, as this bird stood out to me from my office window, leaving them vulnerable to predators. It was a beautiful sight to see, and I felt deep peace in that moment.

THE TRUTH I KNOW NOW

That trait of self-reliance that once defined me—that prideful heart—was so far from God. It marked the beginning of many things that would be stripped away so my true identity in Christ could be revived and revealed. *Man does not live on bread alone.*

The dove serves as a symbol of divine presence, purity, and the anointing of the Holy Spirit. Almost five years later, as I write this, the Holy Spirit gave me another revelation of that bird: a metaphor for many Christians who have picked up their cross and committed to walk the righteous narrow path.

Luke 3:22 (NKJV)
And the Holy Spirit descended on him in bodily form like a dove. And a voice came from heaven: You are my Son, whom I love; with you, I am well pleased.

Deuteronomy 8:14–18

Be careful that your heart doesn't become proud, and you forget the Lord your God who brought you out of the land of Egypt, out of the place of slavery. He led you through the great and terrible wilderness with its poisonous snakes and scorpions, a thirsty land where there was no water. He brought water out of the flint rock for you. He fed you in the wilderness with manna, which your ancestors had not known, in order to humble and test you, so that in the end he might cause you to prosper. You may say to yourself, 'My power and my own ability have gained this wealth for me,' but remember that the LORD your God gives you the power to gain wealth, in order to confirm his covenant, he swore to your ancestors, as it is today.

The Quiet Drift

Not having a job at this time was extremely hard for me. I didn't know how to be idle and not moving forward toward something; I didn't know how to not have an income and to sit still in knowing this. Thankfully I was secure enough financially to take time off, though I had to adjust to having leisure time. I love to read so I figured I could get a good amount of reading done during this break. I came across an audiobook entitled *Of Water and Spirit*, which was mind blowing; after I finished the book, I searched for more from the author, and came across *Wisdom from the Heart of Africa*. This book awakened something in me, something that I had been seeking for as long as I could remember. This book at the time made so much sense, it felt so right. I finished the book in one sitting while outside my home on a summer day. I started to implement the idea of connecting with my ancestors.

When I finished the book, I planned to go and meet the author. I wanted to meet and speak with him; he was from Burkina Faso, so I started to plan a trip to West Africa. As I searched for how to get in touch with him, to my surprise, I saw that he was in the U.S. and would be leading a program in a few months. I thought to myself: *This is meant to be*. I went to the webpage to obtain more information and found that it was a five-day retreat, which was more than I was expecting. I was simply looking for a meet-and-greet. However, this retreat seemed to entail much more.

It seemed to be the only way to get to meet him, so I signed up—I didn't have any other connections who knew him. As I looked up the exact location and the application details, I came across the name of the retreat site: *Brittany's Mountain*. For a moment, I was almost creeped out. I don't believe in coincidence—so I signed up. To me, at the time, it felt like a double sign: creepy, but double clear.

I signed up for the upcoming retreat, which was called the Elemental Immersion. This was the only class which required no prerequisite of prior understanding. I asked my husband to join me, but he was not feeling the cost for this retreat. He wanted to join me as a moral supporter at no cost (he's funny!).

At this point, I'm signed up and excited, and there are roughly six months before the retreat. In that time, I read all his books. I started to entertain the notion of our ancestors being helpers in our lives once they have passed on and that nature and its elements also play a role in helping us in this realm. It wasn't far-fetched to me: it felt right, it made sense, and there was a part of me that wanted to believe it.

To be clear, I never stopped believing in God Almighty. I took this as having extra helpers, as a bonus: an expansion of my belief. I put this new practice of speaking and asking for support from my ancestors to the test. I created an ancestor shrine and every morning I would put fresh water in a small dish, a libation, and light a tea candle for them. I would also sit and talk to them from time to time; it was very therapeutic. If only I had known the fire I was stepping into.

I'm practical when it comes to things like this and one day

I said: *All right, ancestors, it's time for me to get back to work.* I was fortunate enough to have options when returning to the workforce. I took the top three companies that I wanted to work for and had landed interviews with them. After the interviews I wrote down the salary range I wanted for each company. I placed them on my ancestor shrine and asked them to help make this happen. I received an email from one of my top three picks and an offer letter came shortly after with the maximum number that I had written on my salary range request. I read the offer letter thinking that somehow they must have made a mistake. My husband and I looked at each other, he breaks the silence by saying, "I told you this is where you would be: congratulations!" It was one of the most memorable days of that time in my life. I told my husband what I had asked for, down to the overly hopeful maximum range, and there it was. I thanked my ancestors. I was excited and ready to get back to work. The time off was nice, but I was ready to get back in the game.

THE TRUTH I KNOW NOW

As the old saying goes: "An idle mind is the devil's playground."

Proverbs 9:16–18
"Whoever is inexperienced, enter here!" To the one who lacks sense, she says, "Stolen water is sweet, and bread eaten secretly is tasty!" But he doesn't know that the departed spirits are there, that her guests are in the depths of Sheol.

> **Exodus 20:2–4**
> I am the LORD your God, who brought you out of the land of Egypt, out of the place of slavery. Do not have other gods besides me. Do not make an idol for yourself, whether in the shape of anything in the heavens above or on the earth below or in the waters under the earth. Do not bow in worship to them, and do not serve them; for I, the LORD your God, am a jealous God.

The retreat trip quickly approached. I scheduled the time off in advance with the job for this trip as part of the acceptance offer. The night before I was scheduled to leave, I started to get cold feet. We planned to head out the next morning around 6 a.m. and make it a road trip—the location was about a thirteen-hour drive from my home.

The morning came and I did not want to go. I had never been to a retreat before, and I had never stayed overnight among people I didn't know. In that moment, it all felt crazy to me. My husband was very supportive, in trying to talk me through my fears and reminded me of how certain and excited I'd been when planning the trip. He said he would take me to and from the place so that I didn't have to stay overnight if I didn't feel comfortable. This made me feel a little better about going, but I was still not one hundred percent.

I went upstairs and spoke to my ancestors—specifically my paternal grandmother Gross, or so I thought at the time. I asked for a sign of confirmation to go. My husband was outside in the car waiting on my final decision. I gathered the last of my things, dragging my feet with each step. When I finally made it outside and opened the car door, the song "I Will Be There" by Odessa was playing. The hook—"I will be there, standing by your side"—was coming through the speakers, and in that moment, I felt a deep assurance that everything would be okay. It was as if my grandmom was reminding me that she would be there with me.

DISCLAIMER

Before going into the detail of these practices, I want to be clear: if I had known what I was truly getting myself into, I would have stayed far away from it. These practices are extremely dangerous—you do not know who you are speaking or communing with. We may like to believe it's our loved ones and that we are safe, but the truth is that unclean spirits and demons only come to kill, steal, and destroy. They are cunning and deceitful. There is absolutely nothing good that can come from this—nothing worth the cost of your soul and separation from the Creator, God Almighty.

Elemental Immersion: Seeking Power in Nature
(West African Dagara Cosmology)

ARRIVAL AT BRITTANY'S MOUNTAIN

My husband drove me and stayed nearby; the hotel was about five minutes away. The plan was for him to pick me up after the events each evening and bring me back in the morning. I paid for a room at the retreat, that I decided to forfeit—and that was completely fine with me. I went in with a plan: to meet the author and sit through this retreat, and nothing more. I packed my own food and water, and each night my husband picked me up before coming back in the morning. I still wasn't comfortable with the idea of sleeping among people I didn't know.

DAY 1: SETTLE-IN

The house was nice, with plenty of land surrounding it. A man and woman greeted me at the door when we pulled up. Their welcome was warm, and I remember looking at the woman and thinking how much she resembled my aunt—right down to her mannerisms. I walked inside and there were many people there; everyone seemed to be doing their own thing, getting settled in. They were chatting cheerfully, laughing, and moving about with ease; it seemed like they all knew each other already. I, on the other hand, was still trying to figure out how to be in this environment. It all felt new and uncomfortably strange to me. As I made my way into the kitchen to find the person in charge, I ran into a woman who looked to be about my age. We greeted each other with big smiles, smiles so big you would have thought we were reconnecting after a long separation. We exchanged names, it was strange, and so sudden—like I had momentarily stepped into the same cheerful rhythm as everyone else. After the encounter I remember thinking: *Oh no, I'm catching whatever everyone else is on in this place.*

The first day followed a standard "meet and share" circle format. We were told that this would be the routine and flow each morning: a personal sharing round, followed by the agenda for the day. I sat there wondering how I was possibly going to make it through five days of this. The share circle started, and everyone took turns introducing themselves and sharing why they had come.

I felt like I stood out, that I was an impostor. I didn't know that culture, and I didn't know what it meant to be "indigenous and free." I was proper, reserved, and focused only on the reason I was there. I was seeking truth—what was this way of life and why had it drawn me here? It was somewhat comforting to hear from another older woman who admitted she had also come with strong hesitation, nearly backing out at the last minute. That gave me a sense of relief, a reminder that I wasn't entirely alone in my unease.

I made it through the meet-and-greet. When the day

concluded, my husband was waiting just outside at our scheduled pickup time to bring me back to our place for the night.

> **THE TRUTH I KNOW NOW**
>
> John 14:6 (KJV)
> Jesus saith unto him, I am the way, the truth, and the life: no man cometh unto the Father, but by me.

DAY 2: EARTH

The next day, I returned to the house in time for the morning share circle. The host began in the same format as the day before—going around the room for people to share. It could be a dream from the night before, questions about the ritual, whatever was on your mind, or nothing at all.

Some of the red-flag dreams that stood out to me were: *"Dream of a church—people shaking and screaming, and Bible pages burning. There is a point of no return. Are you willing to go?"* Another person shared that in their dream they were told to *"get ready to embrace your death."* Hearing these two dreams shared made me uneasy. I looked around the room at peoples' expressions: like, is anyone hearing this, anyone concerned? But no one reacted. When the dream about Bible pages burning and the point of no return was shared, I asked the person what her response had been—did she say yes or no? I needed more context. What exactly are we talking about? Why was everyone treating it so casually?

I didn't have any dream to share this morning. But I knew that if I had dreamed anything like what I had just heard, that would've been it—I would have ended my retreat right there and gone home with my husband and Sav. After everyone shared, the spiritual teacher gave his take on the dreams and shares, then shifted us toward the day's ritual. Some of his statements stayed with me: *"Sometimes light masquerades as shadow. The power of the shadow is its capacity to masquerade as light. Knowing light is more appealing than shadow and darkness. More are attracted to light. ... Look down at if a person casts a shadow or not, if you do not see a person's shadow that is a disembodied entity."*

From that point on, any time we stepped outside, my eyes were on the ground. Then he shared more that unsettled me. *"Otherworldly adversaries will never do what they do to you unless you are carrying something so important that they cannot turn their back at. Attention is bestowed upon those that carry something of interest. ... Spiritual gifts can be 'snatched' and you won't know, occupied by entities unbeknown to you, leading people to do things completely nonsensical human-wise."*

THE TRUTH I KNOW NOW

2 Corinthians 11:14–15
For Satan disguises himself as an angel of light. So it is no great surprise if his servants also disguise themselves as servants of righteousness.

> **John 10:10**
> A thief comes only to steal and kill and destroy. I have come so that they may have life and have it in abundance.
>
> **1 John 4:1**
> Dear friends, do not believe every spirit, but test the spirits to see if they are from God.
>
> **Ephesians 6:12**
> For our struggle is not against flesh and blood, but against the rulers, against the authorities, against the cosmic powers of this darkness, against evil, spiritual forces in the heavens.

The Spiritual Teacher's Preparation for Earth Ritual

The teacher spoke of a disconnection from earth and a disrespect of the feminine, saying that this ritual would bring us back to the womb of the mother, to return to earth. He declared, "Mother knows it all." His idea was to deepen one's verification of the sanctity of "Mother Earth," the very ground we walk on every day. He said we should consciously deliver respect to the earth, which sustains our very breath in this dimension. He continued: *"Return to the earth like a baby in the womb. It's the mind in which you are in that makes all the difference. There needs to be a new perspective to look at it from a different angle and realize that the best healer we have is the one that we walk on every day."*

Elemental Immersion: Seeking Power in Nature

THE TRUTH I KNOW NOW

There has been a disconnect from our Creator, God Almighty. He deserves our full respect and reverence, for He is the one true Healer.

Genesis 1:1–3
In the beginning God created the heavens and the earth. Now the earth was formless and empty, darkness covered the surface of the watery depths, and the Spirit of God was hovering over the surface of the waters. Then God said, "Let there be light" and there was light."

Genesis 2:7
Then the Lord God formed the man out of the dust from the ground and breathed the breath of life into his nostrils, and the man became a living being.

Acts 17:25 (KJV)
He giveth to all life, and breath, and all things.

Back to the Earth Ritual Preparation Share

The teacher continued:

> *Give honor to ourselves, our authority, our belonging. By doing that, our identity becomes manifested. Those entities that once looked like us are now working with the earth.*

> *They want to work with us to increase the level of awareness to the critical mass in order for the ultimate message to be delivered that needs to be executed in order to begin a massive healing.*
>
> *Imagine people joining everywhere in concert. Singing a song of praise to the earth mother. Something yet to be known but will be known at that particular time. Making people thousand miles apart be in the same environment. That is what is going to heal. It is important that we bow to it. And in the process by calling all the invisible forces to come and join us to humbly kneel to the mother being by asking: please forgive us, I didn't know what I was doing.*

Listening back to these recordings, I almost burst into laughter. But in these moments, it wasn't funny. I had been sitting there in that environment, listening to this nonsense. It was disturbing on so many levels. I rebuke these lies, and every ear that heard it, in the mighty name of Jesus Christ—lies from the deepest pits of Sheol.

THE TRUTH I KNOW NOW

Satan wants so badly to be God. He is still trying—but his time, in perverting God's Word and causing chaos, is coming to an end. His days are numbered. He is nothing more than a mimicker—a creation, not the Creator. We, God's children, bow in worship and praise only to God Almighty. We give no honor to ourselves, but to our Father in heaven and to our Lord and Savior, Jesus Christ, who died for our sins and rose on the third day.

> **Revelation 12:9,12**
> So the great dragon was thrown out—the ancient serpent, who is called the devil and Satan, the one who deceives the whole world. He was thrown to earth, and his angels with him. Therefore rejoice, you heavens, and you who dwell in them! Woe to the earth and the sea, because the devil has come down to you with great fury, because he knows his time is short.

> **Deuteronomy 12:30–31**
> Be careful not to be ensnared by their ways after they have been destroyed before you. Do not inquire about their gods, asking, "How did these nations worship their gods?" You must not do the same to the LORD your God, because they practice every detestable act, which the LORD hates, for their gods.

> **Luke 23:34 (KJV)**
> Then Jesus said, "Father, forgive them; for they know not what they do."

The Earth Ritual

That night, during the ritual, we were all lying on our backs on the ground, looking up at the night sky, with the intention of being "held by the earth" and with a sense of being "reborn." Each person had a watcher to help them in and out of the hole, or if attention was needed while in it. I remember during the digging process seeing many baby spiders on the ground. A lady picked one up and identified them as baby wolf spiders. That was enough for me—there was no way I was lying down on the ground, especially at night. My group reassured me that our hole had been triple-checked and cleared of anything that crawls, but still, I was the last one to enter. While lying in the ground all I could focus on was whether something was crawling on me, ready to leap out at the first sign of movement. I tried to distract myself, looking up at the vast sky—it was beautiful. The night air grew cold quickly, and I was ready to get out.

I remembered the host had said that we would know when the ritual was complete—either "they" would tell us, or we would "just know." I decided my sign would be feeling embraced, how would I feel this—I didn't know, but that was the sign I decided on. My thinking was that I was probably not going to "get" or "hear" what they hear, so my confirmation will be feeling embraced.

When I climbed out, my legs felt weak, almost useless. I hadn't been in the hole long enough for them to fall asleep, but for a moment I was scared. At that instant, two women I had bonded with during the retreat—women who felt like aunties—embraced me. One wrapped me in a blanket from the front, the other held me from behind. They guided me to the fire, where people sat in silence, some crying, some weeping deeply. I wondered what they were experiencing.

By the time we finished, it was late. My husband was waiting faithfully outside, though the service was terrible, and calls and texts barely went through. The host again warned me of the "danger" of leaving after such a radical ritual—of stepping outside the set perimeter of safety. She insisted she needed to know where we were staying so she could "protect our travel." I brushed it off, but I did feel elevated, unsure of what I had just experienced.

The drive back to our place was intense. Darkness and heavy fog swallowed the road, and our headlights were our only guide. The GPS didn't work in the remote area, so we drove from my memory. At one turn, I saw something in the road. *"Watch out—something's there,"* I told my husband. It was a dog—not a stray, but a well-groomed, collared dog. It stood perfectly still in the darkness until our headlights illuminated it. Then it barked once and darted into the darkness. The whole sight was surreal. I didn't want to scare or alarm my husband, but I knew something was off.

Moments later, I glanced to my left—and we were back at the retreat. My stomach dropped. How had we ended up here again? It was as if we drove in a circle. I stayed composed, not wanting to unsettle my husband further, but in my spirit, I knew that magic and incantations were at play.

DAY 3: FIRE

I arrived back at the retreat just in time for the morning share circle. Listening back to the recording, I noticed that many people referred to the hole as a grave. I thought: *That's a pretty accurate description.*

Morning Share Circle

I shared the dream I'd had the night before, as well as my morning experience. The night prior, after the earth ritual and into the morning, I had a headache. I rarely, if ever, get headaches, so I wasn't sure what caused it. That morning, before I made it back to the retreat, my Mom called me early in the morning to check in. She didn't know the details of the retreat (I wouldn't have been there if she had), and just wanted to see how I was doing. She said she was running late for work, which was unusual. When I asked if everything was okay, she told me she had woken up dizzy, and it had taken her longer than usual to get ready. A mother will forever be connected to her child.

I also shared my dream. I couldn't remember all of it, but what I did recall was something pulling me down. I was trying to go up, and whatever it was that was pulling me was slipping. I tried shaking it off, but it wouldn't let go. I could feel its grip; it still had hold of me. It was pulling me by my feet.

> **THE TRUTH I KNOW NOW**
>
> Proverbs 3:25–26
> Don't fear sudden danger or the ruin of the wicked when it comes, for the Lord will be your confidence and will keep your foot from a snare.

Ritual Preparation

Before we moved into ritual preparation, a woman in share circle asked: *"What if someone's ancestral purpose was to be a destructive force? Because obviously there are forces of creation and forces of destruction and there has to be some people who come into this life to do destructive things."*

The host replied: *"People may act that way but, in this cosmology, if an ancestor is acting out, they are trying to get someone's attention for healing. They are asking and no one is listening. The ancestors that will show up at the portal, there's no evil that is going to be in this space. And there are no ancestors in the cosmology that are evil. There are ancestors that are in pain and need help."* The host went on to explain: *"If there is an entity that is around or attached to you, then a sweep ritual is performed to remove it and return you to your natural state. I know as soon as you cross my driveway what entities come with you and which entities are in this room."*

The woman pressed further: *"So that means we are all good, no entities are attached to us?"* The reply: *"No, some of you have them but it's your job to clean them up, not mine. Now, if they start f'ing with the group, I will dismiss them. And I tell them up front you can hang out, as long as you don't mess with anyone here."*

The Fire Ritual

That day's ritual involved writing down all your worries and problems on brown paper, then adorning it with flowers, leaves—whatever you could find from nature. Each person tied their items together into a bundle, which would later be thrown into the fire. It was said that the fire served as a barrier between realms, with our ancestors standing on the other side, and that fire could also serve as a portal to see spirits from other realms. Throwing the bundle into the fire symbolized giving your problems over to your ancestors for help.

Three massive fires were set up—one in the center, one to the left, and one to the right. Each person approached the center, delivered their bundle, spoke their piece, and then returned to the group. As they came back, the rest of the group were to welcome them with cheering and hugging—a symbolic "welcome back to the village."

Some people there seemed like veterans. They came prepared with clothes and gadgets for each ritual. I felt like a fish out of water. When it was my turn, I went up and knelt in front of the fire, like the others before me had done. The heat was so intense I thought my eyebrows had gotten singed. Strangely, I felt it mostly on my right side and back, even though the flames surrounded me on nearly all sides. But I didn't see anything. I wanted to. I wanted to know what had drawn me there. I wanted to see what others claimed they could see.

A rehearsed song, accompanied by constant drumming, played throughout the ritual. When I returned from the fire, I didn't get the elaborate "welcome back to the village" that others had. Maybe people were tired from the endless singing and drumming, I thought. Or maybe it was because I didn't stay overnight and bond with them.

THE TRUTH I KNOW NOW

I smile now when I think about it. That wasn't my village. Perhaps that's why they didn't welcome me as one of their own. At that time, I was still a lost sheep wandering in the wilderness. This ritual demonstrated another mimicry of the Word: handing your problems and worries to ancestors as if God Almighty isn't sufficient.

Psalm 55:22

Cast your burden on the LORD, and he will sustain you; he will never allow the righteous to be shaken.

Matthew 11:28–30

"Come to me, all of you who are weary and burned, and I will give you rest. Take up my yoke and learn from me, because I am lowly and humble in heart, and you will find rest for your souls. For my yoke is easy and my burden is light."

Isaiah 8:19

When they say to you, "Inquire of the mediums and the spiritist who chirp and mutter," shouldn't a people inquire of their God? Should they inquire of the dead on behalf of the living? Go to God's instruction and testimony! If they do not speak according to this word, there will be no dawn for them.

Back to the Story

By the end of the ritual, it was extremely late. I was tired and had told my husband it was okay and that I would stay this night. I asked him to bring me some things to get me through the night. He asked a million times if I was sure, and if I was under some type of manipulation. Thinking back now, it's very possible. But I stayed.

The host showed me to a room in which I shared with two other women. I stayed up awhile, chatting with a few people, then I went up for bed. I could not sleep. I lay awake in the dark, staring—it was so dark I couldn't even see if something was right in front of me. I kept hearing a sound like a siren, constantly—like a fire truck being dispatched. I thought, *How can anyone sleep through this?*

Sometime in the late morning, I finally dozed off for a few hours.

DAY 4: WATER

I got up very early. Only two others were awake. I went downstairs and sat with one of the ladies I had spoken with the day before, later learning she was a very prominent woman in this space. I asked if she had slept well last night, since we shared the same room. She said that she had, and I thought, *Well, that's strange.* I asked if she had heard the noise during the night. She said no. I didn't believe her.

"Are you sure?" I pressed. "It was so loud—like a siren." She shook her head no and asked, "What does that mean to you?" I paused, wasn't sure what she was asking or how to answer as

I thought we all heard it. I asked her for clarity regarding her question, she replied "What does the sound of a siren mean to you?" In that moment, without hesitation, I responded: "Danger."

Morning Share Circle

The first share came from a woman describing her dream:

> My dream was intense. We were all guards at a prison and people were being punished in terrible ways. One of the most significant that confirmed this was earth and here and now, is that one of the people being punished looked like a girl that was in the room. She was wearing all white and was hanging from a tree, her feet were on a chair though, just barely keeping her alive. They were punishing people in all these inhuman ways and eventually they turned into monsters, vampires, werewolves, and horrific creatures. At the end of the dream there were two groups. One was doppelgangers—made from taking pictures of the monsters. There was an army of doppelganger monsters, and they needed to be chopped up and destroyed because they weren't actual people. The second group of people meditated for two hours at a time, it was very specific timing. They projected it—it was like an army of security people. These are the armies and there will be a war.

(Side note: I had to look up the term "doppelganger." It's German—"doppel" means double and "gänger" means goer/walker. A ghostly double or counterpart of a living person.)

I found this dream share deeply disturbing. The second group—the meditators—reminded me of my own introduction on day one. I had shared my second-guessing, my hesitation, and how I had gone back and forth on whether to come, all the way up to stepping through the door. But a part of me needed to know—what was this pull, this curiosity?

I was in a good place in life at that point, happy and content. I found peace through meditation, coping with normal stress and life's challenges. Many others shared deeply personal things—things I will never repeat—and my heart wept for them. I hesitated in my own introduction because I didn't feel I had anything of that caliber to share. And I truly didn't know why I was there, outside of curiosity and my search for purpose and truth.

THE TRUTH I KNOW NOW

If only we knew the true healing available in God and deliverance through our Lord and Savior Jesus Christ ... The siren I heard that morning was my warning before going into this ritual—water.

> **Psalm 41:3**
> The LORD will sustain him on his sickbed; you will heal him on the bed where he lies.

> **Psalm 147:3–6**
> He heals the brokenhearted and bandages their wounds. He counts the number of the stars; he gives

> names to all of them. Our LORD is great, vast in power; his understanding is infinite. The LORD helps the oppressed but brings the wicked to the ground.

Preparation for the Water Ritual

The spiritual teacher explained that water represents reconciliation and purification. Water connects everyone on the planet. For those born of the water, he said, there is the gift of shapeshifting. The host commented on the peace of water: "Go to the bottom of the ocean, and no one can f*** with your peace."

The teacher then shared how, in his village, shamans would walk into the water and disappear for hours, returning only in the evening. He explained how the currency in his village was cowry shells. Divinations and visits to the shamans were paid with these shells, which were then kept in an urn. At the end of the year, the urn must be taken "back to the source" by the shaman. He described the sight of shamans, in the village, walking through the water, urns full of shells balanced in their hands. I couldn't help but think how far removed this was from God.

In preparation for this ritual, we sang another song. Once again, it was explained that during the ritual this song was to be sung without ceasing. The name of the song was "The Dilemma Song." The sound of it was beautiful, but the meaning was haunting. The story was of a hunter facing an impossible moral choice: to save one familiar hand—his wife's or his mother's—while countless others fell. The teacher told how the hunter, returning from a day of providing food for his people, came upon a scene of horror. The villagers were hanging on the edge of a cliff, many already swept away. Seeing him they stretched their hands upward, desperate to be lifted. But each time he saved one, a dozen more slipped away.

Then he saw two familiar hands side by side—his wife's and his mother's. He could only choose one. The story never revealed who he chose. We sang this song on our walk along the countryside path to the lake.

THE TRUTH I KNOW NOW

This part is worth repeating: we all know that an urn holds cremated ashes after death. The urn in this village, holding the cowry shell currency of its people, is then taken down to the pit of the water. I'm pretty sure they aren't meeting up with the Creator down there to deliver their tally counts for the month. What I hadn't known then was I too was at a crossroad in my life: the wide or narrow path, good and evil.

> **Revelation 20:13**
> Then the sea gave up the dead who were in it, and death and Hades delivered up the dead who were in them: and they were judged, each one according to his works.
>
> **Revelation 13:1,4 (KJV)**
> And I stood on the sand of the sea, and saw a beast

> rise up out of the sea, having seven heads and ten horns, and upon his horns ten crowns, and upon his heads the name of blasphemy. The whole earth was amazed and followed the beast. They worshipped the dragon which gave power unto the beast: and they worshipped the beast, saying, "Who is like the beast? Who is able to make war with him?"
>
> **Hosea 4:6 (KJV)**
> My people are destroyed for lack of knowledge.
>
> **Matthew 7:13–14**
> "Enter through the narrow gate. For the gate is wide and the road broad that leads to destruction, and there are many who go through it. How narrow is the gate and difficult the road that leads to life, and few find it."

The Water Ritual

At the lake, each person went into the water in order, oldest to youngest. When it was my turn, I hesitated, thinking about whether there were snakes in the water. There were two helpers that stayed stationed in the water to hold onto the person going under. During ritual preparation, it was said that the reason for this was so that the spirits of the water didn't take you. The support staff resembled my family. The one on my left looked like my cousin and the person on my right like my aunt. Because of that, I felt safe with them. They held onto my hands and arms as I stepped forward.

The instructions sound simple: let your body flow with the water—become the water. I was so stiff when going under the first time, all I could think about was the caution given regarding the water spirits "taking you." *Where to?* I wondered. *And would I see these spirits when I went under?* It took me a minute to get settled. Each time I dipped beneath the surface, I opened my eyes to make sure there was nothing around me. At first, it was pitch-black water. But the third time I went under I saw tunnels—yes, tunnels. To my right, there were tunnels stretched out like pathways, or gigantic wormholes, to an unknown place. There in front of my eyes were tunnels like another world hidden beneath the water—it was no longer the lake bottom and dark water that I had seen in the first two dips. In my peripheral vision to the left, I caught sight of white light. It was far in the distance, beaming through the darkness, steady and unmoving. It was shining through the water.

When I came out the water, the group embraced me and wrapped me in a warm blanket while the next person was called forward. I sat there, with what I just experienced, not really understanding what it meant. Then the girl next to me nudged me, pointing. "Look, look—do you see that portal?"

At first, I wasn't sure what she meant, and I was still thinking of what I had just seen. When I looked off in the distance to where she was pointing, nestled in the trees near the forest, I saw it: a round hole, like an opening to another place. It was a portal. I lifted my eyes to the sky and another portal was open in the sky. Strangely, I wasn't afraid. In that moment, I understood that there was much more to our reality than what we know and can see.

> **THE TRUTH I KNOW NOW**
>
> God was with me.
>
> ### John 1:3–5
> All things were created through him, and apart from him not one thing was created that has been created. In him was life, and that life was the light of men. That light shines in the darkness, and yet the darkness did not overcome it.
>
> ### Psalm 139:7–12
> Where can I go to escape your Spirit? Where can I flee from your presence? If I go up to heaven, you are there; if I make my bed in Sheol, you are there. If I fly on the wings of the dawn and settle down on the western horizon, even there your hand will lead me; your right hand will hold on to me. If I say, "Surely the darkness will hide me, and the light around me will be night"—even the darkness is not dark to you.

LAST DAY OF THE RETREAT

Morning Share Circle

A woman shared her dream:

> I was in a yard with this thing that looked like a mix between a puppet and an executioner. It wore a leather robe like an executioner, it was very fat, and it had a very fat puppet-like head. It was talking to me gently and it said, 'the more I move the more I want to kill.' I was trying to empathize with it, and I started to talk about semantics. As I spoke it took my hand, and tried to take my grandmother's ring off my finger. I bit it and said, 'This isn't for you.' When I bit it, I swallowed part of it along with my grandmother's ring. I woke up terrified, then started convulsing. I didn't know whether this was a dangerous entity, it was 5 a.m. and I didn't know what to do. I was scared.

By the end of the morning share circle, I was mentally drained. I had experienced so much that I had no logical answers for, no clear understanding of what to do with everything I had encountered. Later, while reviewing my notes and recordings, I came across a letter I had written that day to another lady at the retreat. I never sent it.

The Letter

> After the circle gathering on our last day, I was very overwhelmed—emotional, trying to process so much I

couldn't quite understand. I had no room left. I want to thank you for your presence that morning you came out on the deck and sat beside me in the rocking chair. Your grace was like a knowing—like spirit flowed through you in that moment—and I was completely speechless. I had gone outside for fresh air, needed space to think and try to process what I was experiencing. I chose a spot at the far end of the deck—away from everyone. I wanted to cry. I wanted to be alone and clear my mind. Everything I had ever questioned was being revealed in ways that didn't make sense—contradicting everything I thought to be true. You came out, and I tried to pull myself together quickly, expecting you to ask if I was okay or start talking. But to my surprise—silence. It was golden. It was everything I wanted and needed in that moment. So much so that I had to glance over to see who it was sitting beside me. As I slowly peeked to the right, the name of the person sitting next to me was **MERCY**.

THE TRUTH I KNOW NOW

God never left me. He was there through it all. The letter didn't need to be sent—writing it was enough, because God knew this day would come. The girl's name was Mercy. How poetically and beautifully God works. As I look back on this journey, I can see the places God left a little sprinkle of His presence, a reminder of His love, protection, and patience. He never left my side. All glory to the one and only YHWH.

Ephesians 2:4–5
But God, who is rich in **mercy**, because of His great love with which He loved us, even when we were dead in trespasses, made us alive together with Christ.

Ancestralization: Calling on the Ancestors

I was on a roll and had already signed up for the next retreat. At that time, I had no clue that I was only digging myself into a deeper hole. When it came time to go, I felt hesitant again—but this time I drove myself and stayed on-site. This time was different. I walked differently. I walked with many; I could feel it. I wasn't the same person who had arrived at the Elemental Immersion just three months earlier—and I knew it.

DAY 1: MEET AND GATHER

I arrived later than the suggested time—traffic was heavy, and I had to stop at the store for a few things on the way. By the time I made it, everyone was already in the main room, sitting in a circle and sharing. I recognized most of the people from the previous retreat, but there were also many new faces. When I entered, I came in like I owned the place—my energy was big. I felt the atmosphere in the room shift, almost as if the channel turned to my station and everyone was waiting for me to speak. Normally, when that much attention is on me, I shrink back. I'm not an attention seeker, and I usually maneuver around moments like that. But this day, I stayed right where I was—boldly. Naturally, I was next to share since those I knew were already whispering greetings, lip-talking hellos, exchanging air hugs, smiling and giggling with me. It felt good to see everyone again. I found an open seat next to a gentleman I didn't know—he resembled my uncle. I shared about my drive in, including how I had almost been side-swiped off the highway by a tractor-trailer.

After the circle meet-and-greet, the host went into more depth about the retreat, beginning with the elements. She explained that "Elemental Immersion" was a prerequisite to this ancestralization learning. She spoke about each element—earth, water, fire, nature, and mineral—and how we were to come into alignment with them now that we had the understanding and had already gone through the rituals in the first retreat.

She then shared that in the Dagara tribe, it is believed that when a person is born, they are born into a clan with the propensity to carry a certain medicine. At birth, a "yes" is given to the element and clan, signifying the person's willingness to carry its power and medicine. The last number of one's year of birth was said to determine which element you naturally embody or belong to. When something goes wrong in a person's life, it is believed that one or more elements are out of harmony and must be realigned. We went around the group identifying everyone's elements. According to this system, I would be considered fire.

THE TRUTH I KNOW NOW

These entities, beings and unclean (departed) spirits cannot just walk into your life and cause havoc. They require your permission—whether given knowingly or unknowingly—or access through sin, where you step outside of God's covering and covenant.

> **Job 9:4–9,12**
> God is wise and all-powerful. Who has opposed Him and come out unharmed? He removes mountains without their knowledge, overturning them in his anger. He shakes the earth from its place so that it's pillars tremble. He commands the sun not to shine and seals off the stars. He alone stretches out the heavens and treads on the waves of the sea. He makes the stars; the Bear, Orion, the Pleiades, and the constellations of the southern sky. If he snatches something, who can stop Him? Who can ask Him what are you doing?

Back to the Story

After circle, everyone got settled in. I went to bed rather early after chatting and catching up with a few people. I was sharing a room with one woman that I knew from the Elemental Immersion retreat and three others who were new acquaintances—we connected naturally. That night, when I lay down to rest and closed my eyes, I saw the face of a witch—an evil entity. I opened and closed my eyes at least three times, and each time it was there. I prayed and eventually fell asleep.

THE TRUTH I KNOW NOW

What I saw that night when I closed my eyes was what was truly present in the spirit. By God's grace, I was able to discern what was in that place.

> **Matthew 13:16**
> "Blessed are your eyes because they do see, and your ears because they do hear."

DAY 2: ANCESTOR AND EARTH SHRINE

Morning Share Circle

Everyone was up bright and early for morning share circle. I chose not to share what I had seen before going to sleep. In that moment, I didn't want to be the bearer of bad news—that something evil was among us. Nor did I want to offend any of the ladies in the room I was sharing space with. After circle, we were told to be sure to get good rest that night, because the next day we wouldn't sleep again until the following morning. The ancestor ritual was performed overnight outside. The host began teaching on what "ancestralization" meant, preparing us for what was to come.

Ancestralization Explained

In Dagara tradition, ancestralization is the handing over of a loved one to the realm of the ancestors. It involves a series of rituals to aid in the transition or "safely return" the dead to their ancestral home. To the Dagara, it is a duty after someone passes to ensure rest, continuity, and a home for them. The tools required were a stick and a stool, meant to symbolize the male and female ancestors in one's lineage and appoint them as gatekeepers. The stick and stool were said to be physical objects that the ancestors could "come into."

Preparation for the Ritual

For the ritual, we were told we would be creating a village, modeled after Dano, the spiritual teacher's own village. Within this "village" there would be two shrines: an ancestor and earth shrine. The earth shrine was dedicated to *tenbalu*, representing the feminine spirit, and *tingan*, the masculine spirit, was said to represent father earth and is always in the form of a tree. According to the Dagara, when a village is founded, there is always a *tingan* shine—a tree believed to house the spirit that protects the land and people. We were told that the tree acted as an umbrella of protection from negative spirits, entities, and forces in the wild. The female counterpart, *tenbalu*, was compared to what many in the West call Mother Earth. It was also said that *tingan* brings abundance and well-being to all connected to him, though he supposedly only dwells in the Daraga land.

The host shared:

If you think about a tree, it always provides an umbrella of protection over the ones under it. My tingan *shrine here is a tree, but the extension of the umbrella covers the entire property, and its roots are very deep. This* tingan *shrine is connected to the shrine in Dano. Tingan is father earth. And it's about protection, groundedness, and anchoring. It's like the best Dad ever—no one can f*** with* tingan's *kids. When we are aligned, you are protected everywhere you go, because trees are everywhere, and trees have a network underground in the root system.*

THE TRUTH I KNOW NOW

This is one of the most disturbing and dangerous misconceptions anyone could believe. The Creator, God Almighty, is the true Father—the only one worthy of the "best Dad ever" title. Where was I, that I couldn't speak up in that moment, to spark even a single question that might challenge this belief? I will walk with the Creator over any creation. The idea that a spirit in a tree could be omnipresent, or protective is nothing more than a counterfeit—one of the adversary's oldest tricks. The imitation is heartbreaking when the real thing is freely available. Don't settle for less. God is the real deal. God Almighty—Alpha and Omega, the Beginning and the End. He alone is omnipresent, the ultimate protector and provider.

I don't speak as a know-it-all. I was in this mess too, deceived because I didn't know the Word. I wasn't rooted in God's truth. I thought I had God and that was enough. I don't share this to condemn, but to expose the lies of the enemy. True love and protection come only from our Heavenly Father. The effort poured into these practices—building shrines, performing rituals, maintaining spiritual "contracts"—is endless. And it comes with a cost you cannot afford. But with God, you don't need any of that. His grace is sufficient. When He acts, who can reverse it? Through Jesus Christ, we have direct access to the Father—nothing counterfeit, just a firsthand relationship with Him.

> **Isaiah 46:1–2,5**
> Bel bows down; Nebo cowers. Idols depicting them are cosigned to beast and cattle. The images you carry are loaded, as a burden for the weary animal. The gods cower; they crouch together; they are not able to rescue the burden, but they themselves go into captivity. "To whom will you compare me or make me equal? Who will you measure me with, so that we should be like each other?"
>
> **Isaiah 46:9–10**
> Remember what happened long ago, for I am God, and there is no other; I am God, and no one is like me. I declare the end from the beginning, and from long ago what is not yet done, saying: my plan will take place, and I will do all my will.
>
> **Isaiah 66:1**
> This is what the Lord says: "Heaven is my throne, and earth is my footstool. Where could you possibly build a house for me?"

Back to the Story

We were then told we would be doing a "self-divination." While in meditation, we were to ask which ancestor—one male, one female—would come forward for us and simply observe.

To prepare, we did an exercise meant to clear our body,

emotions, and mind of what no longer served us—attitudes, thoughts, beliefs. They called it getting into "the right mental space." Through breath and whatever sound(s) came up for us, we were to release anything stored in the body. I remember thinking, *I've never screamed by myself, let alone a room full of people*. But perhaps this was something I needed. I thought in that moment: *This might even be fun—I could use a good scream*.

My experience was the complete opposite. As people began releasing sounds, I heard something deeper—in the spirit. These weren't just screams. They were cries of ancient pain, hurt, and suffering. My heart broke, and tears filled my eyes for everyone in that room. During the preparation huddle, the host said something that stood out to me: "Your body is sovereign."

THE TRUTH I KNOW NOW

1 Corinthians 6:19–20

Don't you know that your body is a temple of the Holy Spirit who is in you, whom you have from God? You are not your own, for you were bought at a price. So glorify God with your body.

Back to the Story

Following this screaming exercise, we were instructed to move into the self-divination practice. We were told to be open to connecting and working with our ancestors—even if we didn't know them, because "they know you." We were assured that even without knowing their names, we could still call on them and work with them. But this just wasn't sitting right with me—especially after what I just heard in that screaming exercise. I was still shaken and traumatized by the cries and sounds that filled the room. It was hard for me to focus. We sat together in meditation for about 15–20 minutes. I tried to imagine my late uncle and aunt as my chosen "male and female ancestors," but when it came time for us to share, I had nothing. I simply carried on. We were then told to carry out our sticks and stools to the wilderness and leave them overnight.

THE TRUTH I KNOW NOW

When I think back on the things we were told to do—rituals to perform, objects to maintain, practices that were said to be required in order to "help our ancestors" so they could, in turn, help us—was overwhelming. I remember thinking: *My goodness, this feels like a full-time job. Who has time for this?* The truth is, the only way those spirits could do anything for you was if you first did something for them. That's the deal. That's the contract. But God doesn't work that way. He doesn't need anything from us. What could we possibly give our Creator that He doesn't already have?

The amount of time, energy, and effort poured into these rituals and practices never once acknowledged God for who He is—the very One who provides and sustains your every breath. He doesn't require anything from you but you—dusty, messy, and imperfect as we are. People truly believe they have power outside of God. What a dangerous delusion to think that every spell, ritual, and act of sorcery doesn't come at a mighty cost. Don't let the enemy lie to you—he is the very reason for your pain and suffering. He and his agents are the oppressors you seek to be freed from. And here is another truth: Only God Almighty is all-seeing and all-knowing, and only through Jesus Christ, our Lord and Savior, can you be set free.

Acts 17:23–25
For as I was passing through and observing the objects of your worship, I even found an altar on which was inscribed, 'To an Unknown God.' Therefore, what you worship in ignorance, this I proclaim to you. The God who made the world and everything in it—He is LORD of heaven and earth—does not live in shrines made by hands. Neither is he served by human hands, as though he needed anything, since he himself gives everyone life and breath and all things."

1 Kings 18:21
Then Elijah approached all the people and said, "How long will you waver between two opinions? If the LORD is God, follow Him. But if Baal, follow him."

John 8:34
Jesus responded, "Truly I tell you, everyone who commits sin is a slave of sin."

> **2 Peter 2:19**
> They promise them freedom, but they themselves are slaves of corruption, since people are enslaved to whatever defeats them.

DAY 3: THE VIGIL RITUAL

I woke up to a text from one of my closest friends at 6:25 a.m.:

> Grateful rising!! This is the second dream I had of you … the first one you were killed … me, your Dad and Duane [my oldest brother] ran over screaming … It was scary. There were a few of us in a big house … some of the people I couldn't make out, but when I asked what happened, you were reluctant to tell me. I wasn't sure if it was because you just didn't want anyone else to know, or if it was just me … But you told me, and we just hugged and cried for so long!!

Reading this made me freeze, though it didn't surprise me. She and I have always been spiritually connected this way since childhood. We never fully understood it, but no matter the distance between us, we always remained connected. That bond has carried us through many seasons. In that moment, I felt as though I was helping my ancestors. It didn't click yet—the danger I was truly in.

Morning Share Circle

We didn't sleep again until the next morning. At 8 a.m., everyone gathered in the circle for the morning share. I didn't want to speak because I knew my emotion would overtake me—but I shared anyway:

> I didn't get much sleep last night. I tossed and turned most of the night. I couldn't rest knowing my aunt and uncle were out in the wilderness—the dark woods—alone. I thought about my aunt, the one I hoped had come forward as my female ancestor. She died tragically in a hit-and-run accident. There was no family with her—she was alone when she died. I've never spoken about this to anyone before. She wasn't in my life the way I needed or wished she had been. She had her own battles. Still, she held space in my heart. I was in college when it happened and couldn't make it to the funeral. I hadn't realized how much of that weight I carried until this night. I prayed for her and my uncle, but as I tried to rest, my thoughts kept drifting back to her—again, there she was, alone in the dark. I stretched my hand out onto the pillow and returned to the memory of the night she died. I thought about every detail: the darkness, her being alone, how cold and afraid she must have felt in those final moments—fighting to hold on, wishing someone would come back for her. I pictured myself there with her on that road, telling her it was okay. That I was with her. That I loved her. I cried myself to sleep talking to her.

When I lifted my eyes, the room was silent. Still. I saw tears in the eyes of those around me. A woman softly commended me for my strength and bravery, her own tears falling. Until she said it, I didn't see it that way. My only thoughts were about my aunt—her pain, her loneliness, her final moments. My heart poured out for her. I wanted to ease her suffering, if I had the opportunity, in any way I could.

Today was the day. Everything we had prepared for in the days prior was now to be put into action. We spent the morning creating the "village," preparing it for ritual. Everyone was given tasks based on their "element" to bring it together. The elderly men and woman prepared millet and grain balls for the ancestor shrine and gathered food and snacks for later. Once the village was ready, we went out in order—youngest to oldest—to retrieve the ancestors (the sticks and stools) from the wilderness. We were told to nurture, clothe, and care for them gently. This symbolized reviving our ancestors, bringing them from the wilderness without food and nourishment into communion with us.

On the walk back, we carried our sticks and stools in reverse order—oldest to youngest—back to the village to place them on the ancestor shrine. Before nightfall, several rituals took place. One involved offering millet grain balls as food for the ancestor shrine. Another required mud to be placed around our wrists and ankles, said to "draw out toxins." When darkness fell, we gathered around the fire for the vigil ritual—a nightlong communion with our ancestors. We were told it was a time for meditation, soft conversation, quiet reflection, and sharing any songs, thoughts, or dreams that arose. I remember someone starting a rhyming song that quickly carried through the group. It was funny and it lasted a while, bringing some laughter and lightness to pass the time. Still, we had a long night ahead of us. By the time the sun began rising over the mountaintops, I was sure I had done something wrong—I hadn't seen, heard, or felt anything from my ancestors.

> **THE TRUTH I KNOW NOW**
>
> Colossians 2:8
> Be careful that no one takes you captive through philosophy and empty deceit based on human tradition, based on the elements of the world, rather than Christ.

DAY 4: THE VIGIL RITUAL ENDED

The sun rose over the mountains—by 8 a.m. the ritual had ended. I never went to sleep. My spirit kept alerting me that something wasn't right. I was the only one awake, unsure of what it was, only that I knew it was spiritual. I called my husband and saw I had many missed calls. When he answered, I could hear fear in his voice. He told me he had a dream that "they" took me. In the dream, he explained that he and my Dad were coming to find me.

I was now terrified, but I tried to keep my composure. I didn't want to scare him, though I knew in my spirit something was truly off. It was spiritual. I prayed, and in that moment,

I knew what to do. It was as if my spirit knew what to do. I heard the words: "Get up and remember who you are." I went to shower and washed myself thoroughly, from head to toe. My mind kept going back to the ritual where mud was placed around our wrists and ankles—it hadn't sat right with me then, and it was even louder in my spirit now. In that moment, I remembered I had a cowry shell bracelet that I brought with me from home. I've had it forever—I didn't know where it came from originally or why I brought it with me, but I had a knowing in this moment to get it from my bag. I went back to the ritual space and broke the bracelet there on a rock while speaking words of disagreement and protection over myself. I was physically and spiritually breaking and reversing whatever had been done in that ritual with my words. As I heard myself speaking, I thought, *Who is this woman? She is so powerful.* When I finished, I returned to the house.

Morning Share Circle

People were beginning to wake up and stir. I sat with myself for a while before joining the morning share circle. One share caught my attention this morning. Someone used the name Yeshua. At the time, I didn't know Jesus by this name, so it went right over my head. His name wasn't used in a blasphemous way, but I now recognize it was part of the confusion—mixing His holy name into a practice that wasn't of Him. For God says: "What fellowship does light have with darkness? And what agreement does Christ have with Belial?" The person had been speaking of Yeshua's trait of communing with people, and how she shared that same trait. I pray that Yeshua brings her into truth.

> ### **THE TRUTH I KNOW NOW**
>
> **Proverbs 18:21**
> Death and life are in the power of the tongue, and those who love it will eat its fruit.
>
> **2 Corinthians 6:14–16**
> Do not be yoked together with those who do not believe. For what partnership is there between righteousness and lawlessness? Or what fellowship does light have with darkness? What agreement does Christ have with Belial? Or what does a believer have in common with an unbeliever? And what agreement does the temple of God have with idols? For we are the temple of the living God.

Back to the Story

After the morning share, the host walked us through the agenda for the day—it was the final ritual of the retreat: a chicken sacrifice for the ancestors. We were told that the "ancestors," represented by the stick and stool, had been "revived" and were now strong enough to receive the offering. The logic given was that, just like you wouldn't feed someone a steak after starvation, it must be gradual. It made sense; the first task was to write or speak aloud areas where we needed help within this life.

Phrases I remember hearing:

"You're not asking for the things you need—you are telling them. And you're tasking them with the things you need help with."

"Eventually you may work with other allies—*kontumblé*, *wedamé*, genies, or otherworldly beings. But the ancestors, in this cosmology, are the umbrella or the overseers. So, you know, I have like ten allies, but the ancestors know what's going on—like all the contracts I'm making. They have the big picture; they are involved in all of it."

"Blood is the thing that crosses the barrier the most intensely and quickest so that there is really no barrier."

"Don't transpose the judgmental God of the oppressive culture onto your ancestors. Don't colonize your ancestors with the BS."

THE TRUTH I KNOW NOW

God's Word does not return void. His will *will* be done. Therefore, my brothers and sisters in Christ, put on the full armor of God everyday so you may be able to stand against the schemes of the devil.

> **Romans 6:16**
> Don't you know that if you offer yourselves to someone as obedient slaves, you are slaves of that one you obey—either of sin leading to death or of obedience leading to righteousness.
>
> **Ephesians 6:12 (KJV)**
> For we wrestle not against flesh and blood, but against principalities, against powers, against the rulers of the darkness of this world, against spiritual wickedness in high places.

The Stick and Stool Ritual

The ritual began with us "speaking" to our ancestors through the stick and stool. We were to share and task them with the things we wanted help with—what we wanted to be manifested. For me, this felt awkward. At that point in my life, I wasn't lacking anything physical. I had accomplished what I set my mind to—I was searching for something deeper. I wondered if it was really them—if they were okay, and what life was like where they were. As I sat there, a grasshopper landed on my stick. It startled me, but instantly I had a knowing, a "quantum leap forward." I didn't understand why, but then it hopped onto my stool. My uncle, in life, had been lazy—we loved him, but it was true. Part of me thought maybe this was his way of saying he was going to "hop to it" this time, and I giggled to myself. Meanwhile, as we all individually talked to our "ancestors," the support staff circled, constantly tapping each person's stick and stool with the knife that would soon be used in the chicken sacrifice—said to "keep the ancestors' attention." Then we gathered in a wide circle, shoulder to shoulder, our sticks and stools before us. It was time for the sacrifice.

The Sacrifice

It was a raw sight. When the chicken was cut, I felt a powerful force—like a rushing, weighted wind. I went into a full vision and saw a tunnel—like a time portal. Everything around me faded, and as the portal moved at lighting speed, I began seeing images flashing by, like a movie reel or a time capsule. It was so intense that I couldn't fully understand it, but I tried to hold onto everything I saw so I could document it. When it ended, I turned to the person behind me—we both asked simultaneously, "Did you feel that?" He had felt the force but hadn't seen the visions I saw.

I quickly grabbed my notebook to record everything. Meanwhile, the host held the chicken upside down, walking and dripping its blood on the sticks and stools. She began speaking to individuals, as if relaying messages only she could hear. When she reached me, she looked at me and said, "Speak your truth." I didn't know what she meant, but it stayed with me. Was I not living my truth? Speaking my truth? What is my truth?

Afterward, everyone plucked feathers from the chicken—using its blood as adhesive to place them on their sticks and stools. Some even tucked feathers behind their ears and in their hair. I stood watching, thinking about how unsanitary it was—all the bacteria, lice, and pathogens I was sure were running wild on that thing. The chicken was later cooked and eaten.

THE TRUTH I KNOW NOW

This is dangerous. One of the enemy's many tricks is to divide and distort the truth. God is not the oppressor—He is the only one who brings true freedom from oppression. You may feel or think you are free, but it's just an illusion of the enemy. These practices and sacrifices feed the demons and entities that you are communing with, and you will eventually see who serves who.

2 Corinthians 3:17
Now the LORD is the Spirit, and where the Spirit of the LORD is there is freedom.

Deuteronomy 18:10–12
No one among you is to sacrifice his son or daughter in the fire, practice divination, tell fortunes, interpret omens, practice sorcery, cast spells, consult a medium or a spiritist, or inquire of the dead. Everyone who does these acts is detestable to the LORD.

DAY 5: LAST DAY AT THE RETREAT

This portion of the book was daunting and difficult for me to relive. Even knowing the truth now, I think about all the people I met and all the love that was present—they were genuinely good people. Part of me went through a stage of anger, upset at how deceitful and cunning the enemy can be. I pray for the others; I pray that Jesus finds them just as He found me. I had lost my way, thinking I was moving toward truth. When one engages in such rituals and practices, no matter how innocent they may seem, portals are opened—and there will be a response from the spirit realm, often a response we are not prepared for, nor fully able to understand or control, despite what we may think.

I pray for all the souls I encountered there—for the people I connected with and for the many that I didn't connect with. Their hearts and intentions were good. Many were genuinely good people, professionals and authors. The Holy Spirit has shown me that it doesn't matter how many letters follow your name: Lucifer led one-third of the angels astray. Don't think you can outsmart, outrun, or negotiate with the enemy. Without God, you will fail.

THE TRUTH I KNOW NOW

Listening back to these recordings saddens me, knowing that so many fall victim to this. People are searching and people are hurting. And people who are not grounded in God's Word are taken for a ride from which many never return. I was on that rollercoaster, and I never want to be separated from my God again. I had indeed met my mountain that season. Brittany's Mountain was a monster—a device designed to take me out. I thank God for Jesus Christ, for it was my mustard seed of faith that got me through that experience—nothing is impossible when you have faith. I think about the many souls being misguided and endangered. I pray for those who entered it ignorantly, that God shines His light on them. And for those who knowingly went into the depths, I pray that God has mercy on their souls.

Revelation 12:10
Then I heard a loud voice in heaven say, "The salvation and the power and the kingdom of our God and the authority of his Christ have now come, because the accuser of our brothers and sisters, who accuses them before our God day and night, has been thrown down. They conquered him by the blood of the Lamb and by the word of their testimony; for they did not love their lives to the point of death."

Matthew 17:20
"For truly I tell you, if you have faith the size of a mustard seed, you will tell this mountain, move from here to there, and it will move. Nothing will be impossible for you."

Isaiah 55:6–7
Seek the LORD while he may be found; call to Him while he is near. Let the wicked one abandon his way and the sinful one his thoughts; let him return to the LORD, so He may have compassion on him, and to our God, for He will freely forgive.

The Gift of Prophecy: Vision and Foresight

God blessed me with many gifts, one of which is foresight through vision and dreams. I struggled with this in my youth, unsure of what it was. As I grew older, so did this gift. It matured and it became increasingly difficult to ignore. In the next few chapters, I will share a glimpse into some of my dreams and visions that are relevant to this journey. I was very intentional in selecting which dreams and visions to share, praying for guidance and confirmation. Not everything that the Holy Spirit reveals is meant to be shared.

1 Corinthians 12:7–11 *(simplified attribution)*
A manifestation of the Spirit is given to each person for the common good: to one is given a message of wisdom through the Spirit, to another, the message of knowledge by the same Spirit, to another, faith, gifts of healing, performing miracles, prophecy, distinguishing between spirits, different kind of tongues. One and the same Spirit is active in all of these, distributing to each person as he wills.

Matthew 13:34–35
Jesus told the crowds all these things in parables, and he did not tell them anything without a parable, so that what was spoken through the prophet might be fulfilled: "I will open

my mouth in parables. I will declare things kept secret from the foundation of the world."

God does not expose your spirit to what it cannot handle. Engaging in ungodly practices and rituals exposes you to realms outside of God's Kingdom and covenant, that was never intended for you. Your spiritual eyes become open to these spaces, and in those realms, there are no rules—you are in the wild. And the enemy *will* come to kill, steal, and destroy when you least expect it. No matter what lies he tells you, these agreements come with a cost you cannot afford. It is dangerous to operate outside of the LORD's covenant. I encourage you to pray for spiritual discernment so that you are not deceived by the perceived innocence or trends of the world. The enemy is an imitator, a deceiver of light, whose goal is to steal your faith and destroy you.

(Disclaimer: I leave my dreams in their natural state, unpolished, as long as they are legible. Each word recorded usually holds significance as is.)

VISION: LION AND LIONESS

While in bed preparing to rest, I went into a vision. I saw the faces of a Lion and a Lioness. At first, I thought it was Sav's face, as she resembles a lioness, but the images kept shifting quickly. They were all forward facing until the final vision paused in clear focus: the right-side profile of the Lion's head and mane. It was vivid, steady, and stunningly beautiful. It looked like this:

During that season, I would often search online for the meaning of such dreams and visions. I had no one to commune with, no one to help cultivate the gifts God had given me. Little did I know, the Holy Spirit had been there with me all along, waiting. Looking back now, I understand the danger of seeking interpretation outside of God's Word. Go to Him in prayer and He will reveal.

John 14:26
But the Counselor, the Holy Spirit, whom the Father will send in my name, will teach you all things and remind you of everything I have told you.

Galatians 1:1
Paul, an apostle—not from men or by man, but by Jesus Christ and God the Father who raised him from the dead.

Some time later, I came across a prophecy written by a woman named Helen Calder that had been shared with a church. When I read it, I was immediately reminded of the Lion vision.

I encountered it long after documenting this dream, and when I did, an unexplainable joy filled me. It was refreshing and a reminder that the body of Christ is united and working together for the greater good of the Kingdom of Heaven. More than that, it testified that God's Word never returns void. It stands the test of time—living, active, and still reaching the people He intends, in the exact moment He ordains. She writes: "I saw you passing through a zone of the Presence of God, like a baptism into the cloud, and emerging out the other side with the faces of lions."[1]

THE TRUTH I KNOW NOW

This vision was beautiful, but it also revealed that there was still much work to be done. I was on my way back to God, but the path was not yet clear. The Book of Joel teaches us about the prophet Joel's urgent call for God's people to repent—because without true repentance, there can be no restoration.

God was showing me who I am in spirit, yet I still needed to return fully to Him. It is only in His glory that we gain true perspective—on who we are, on the transformation that comes from His presence, and on the authority, we carry in the name of Jesus Christ. The Lion I saw was a reminder of the tribe of Judah.

---

1 "Prophetic Insight: Greatness, Glory, and the Faces of Lions," https://www.enlivenpublishing.com/2013/07/30/prophetic-insight-the-faces-of-lions/

> **2 Corinthians 3:17–18**
> Now the Lord is the Spirit, and where the Spirit of the Lord is, there is freedom. We all, with unveiled faces, are looking as in a mirror at the glory of the Lord and are being transformed into the same image from glory to glory: this is from the Lord who is the Spirit.
>
> **1 Chronicles 12:8,14**
> Some Gadites joined David at his stronghold in the wilderness. They were valiant warriors, trained for battle, expert with shield and spear. Their faces were like the faces of lions, and they were as swift as gazelles on the mountains. These Gadites were army commanders; the least of them was a match for a hundred, and the greatest of them for a thousand.

DREAM AND VISION: SPIRITUAL THEFT AND THE DOOR

One summer, I connected with a Reiki energy practitioner who later appeared in my dream. She told me to focus, to look into the mirror, and that my spirit guides would show me a message. When I looked, I saw nothing at first—only Savannah by my side.

"Focus," she said again.

As I did, the mirror and the room began to glow a soft sky-blue light. Then, before my eyes, my reflection changed—I was pregnant, my stomach growing rapidly. I was filled with awe and excitement. But when I turned to share what I saw, she was gone.

> ### THE TRUTH I KNOW NOW
>
> I had unknowingly given the enemy access to my life, not understanding the spiritual consequences of my openness. I believe many things were stolen from me in that season—spiritually, emotionally, and perhaps even physically. I now pray for those people, for they know not what they do. And for those who did—may God have mercy on their souls.
>
> #### Proverbs 9:16–18
> "To the one who lacks sense she says, 'Stolen water is sweet, and bread eaten secretly is tasty!' But he does not know that the dead are there, that her guests are in the depths of Sheol."
>
> #### Joel 2:25 (KJV)
> "I will restore to you the years that the swarming locust hath eaten."

There came a season when I sought clarity about the direction of my life. I turned to my own wisdom and the voices around me, instead of opening the Word of God and seeking His face. One morning in prayer, I saw a vision of a door—standing closed before me. I didn't understand it at the time, I tried to interpret the meaning on my own, searching for answers through reasoning. I didn't yet know that the door symbolized more than a decision—it represented the threshold between truth and deception, between self-reliance and surrender.

THE TRUTH I KNOW NOW

The door was never meant to be opened by my own understanding. It was Christ inviting me to seek Him—the true Door, the only way to wisdom, peace, and restoration.

John 10:9 (KJV)
"I am the door. If anyone enters by Me, he will be saved and will go in and out and find pasture."

Matthew 7:7–8
"Ask, and it will be given to you; seek, and you will find; knock, and the door will be opened to you."

Proverbs 3:5–6 (NKJV)
"Trust in the Lord with all your heart and lean not on your own understanding; in all your ways acknowledge Him, and He shall direct your paths."

DRUM MEDITATION AND GOD'S PROMISE

I flew to Chicago to support my friend in his newly started meditation sessions. He described it as a shamanic, spiritual journey that combined meditation by guided storytelling with a rhythmic environment of drums, bells, and shakers. The class had about 10–12 people, filling the room. To my left sat a man who had also studied under the same spiritual teacher from the Dagara tribe of Burkina Faso. Though we had attended the Elemental Immersion at different times, we connected briefly over our shared experience before the session began.

We all lay down in corpse position—flat on our backs, fully relaxed, with the crowns of our heads facing the instructor. As the drumming started, it took me a moment to be present and settle into the rhythm. He first paid homage to his former teacher, who had taught him drumming, as well as to the teacher who had trained both of us in the indigenous ways of Dagara cosmology.

As my body settled into the rhythm, a thought crossed my mind: *If our teacher's spirit is really present, then let me feel it.* In that very moment, a surge of energy rushed through my body, down my back. My mind's eye filled with flashes of visions: vibrant purple, a rainbow with something beneath it, an arched Moroccan-style doorway, and a mass of ocean water flowing behind white Greek-styled houses. The visions came quickly, one after another. I tried holding as much as I could. When the session ended, I rushed to grab my notebook and recorded everything I could remember.

The next day, as I prepared to travel home, delays left me with extra time. I stopped at a nearby park with a dear friend to catch up. As I was about to leave, I noticed a rainbow in the distance. I froze—this wasn't a rainbow in the sky, but an art fixture. I thought back to the vision the evening before and ran to get my notebook. As I compared my drawing and the notes with what was in front of me, I was stunned—it was the rainbow I had drawn from vision and the 'something beneath it' that was out of focus.

At the time, I didn't have a clue what it meant.

> **THE TRUTH I KNOW NOW**
>
> It was God's promise. I was still wandering during that season, thinking I was right in my own way.
>
> ### Genesis 9:12–17
> The rainbow that I have put in the sky will be my sign to you and to every living creature on earth. I will remind you that I will keep this promise forever. When I send clouds over the earth, and a rainbow appears in the sky, I will remember my promise to you and to all other living creatures.
>
> ### Isaiah 54:8–10 (NKJV)
> "With a little wrath I hid My face from you for a moment; but with everlasting kindness I will have mercy on you," says the LORD, your Redeemer. "For this is like the days of Noah to Me; for as I have sworn that the waters of Noah would no longer cover the earth, so have I sworn that I would not be angry with you, nor rebuke you. For the mountains shall depart and the hills be removed, but My kindness shall not

> depart from you, nor shall My covenant of peace be removed," says the Lord, who has mercy on you.

VISION: EYE OF THE STORM

While sitting, I went into a vision of what looked like the eye of a tornado. *What could that mean?* I wondered. *The perfect storm?* Four months later, I dreamt of a massive whirlpool in the ocean—like a tornado made of water, rising upright before me. From above, I watched it from an aerial view. I could feel its gravitational pull, drawing in everything around it, and fear gripped me.

Throughout the dream I found myself in different places. One was an ancient setting filled with darkness and alligators; these were ancient and massive, and the experience was vivid and unsettling. At the end of it all, I remember a woman's face very clearly. She was Caucasian, with pink undertones, her glossy eyes filled with tears and distress. She spoke to me, advising me about something—but upon waking, I couldn't recall her words.

THE TRUTH I KNOW NOW

At the time, I didn't know what this dream meant, but I knew it needed to be documented. Today, almost three years later, the Holy Spirit revealed the meaning: I was in God's hand. He was carrying me through those storms and those dark places. When the enemy could have taken me out, God held and protected me.

> **Isaiah 41:9–10**
>
> I brought you from the ends of the earth and called you from its farthest corners. I said to you: "You are my servant; I have chosen you; I haven't rejected you. Do not fear, for I am with you, do not be afraid, for I am your God. I will strengthen you; I will help you; I will hold on to you with my righteous right hand."

DREAM: DEPARTED SPIRITS AND THE ANCESTOR SHRINE

In my dream, I heard a chattering sound coming from a door to the left of me. It felt like I was in that "in-between" place between sleep and waking. I tried to wake my husband, but I couldn't move or speak normally—what studies call sleep paralysis. The noise grew louder—voices talking, murmuring, drawing closer—as the door slowly opened. When it finally opened, I saw many people—crowds of them—who felt like family. In that moment, I felt at ease, even happy. It was so vivid, as if I were truly living in another dimension while in that sleep state.

Shortly afterward, I had another dream. Though most of it faded upon waking, one detail was crystal clear: my ancestor shrine. In the dream, every picture frame was facedown.

THE TRUTH I KNOW NOW

As I look back through my dream and vision journals, I feel the weight of shame for how I once praised and thanked my so-called "spirit guides" and "elevated ancestors." How did I get here? I often ask myself. How could I have ever wandered so far from the LORD?

1 Samuel 5:1–4 (KJV)
When the Philistines took the ark of God, they brought it into the house of Dagon and set it by Dagon. And when the people of Ashdod arose early in the morning, there was Dagon, fallen on its face to the earth before the ark of the LORD.

Deuteronomy 18:10–12
No one among you is to sacrifice his son or daughter in the fire, practice divination, tell fortunes, interpret omens, practice sorcery, cast spells, consult a medium or a spiritist, or inquire of the dead. Everyone who does these acts is detestable to the LORD.

DREAM: JESUS HID ME IN THE WILDERNESS

During a road trip through New Hampshire and Vermont with my husband and Savannah, I had many dreams. We stayed in a well-known bed-and-breakfast inn. Though it felt a little eerie, I didn't think much of it. The first night, I dreamt I was running through the woods—it felt like a maze. I came to a wooden gate, and as I reached for it, I saw a huge wolf walking toward me. It didn't notice me, so I slowly backed away and knelt down behind the wooden fence. The wolf lingered as if it knew I was—or would be—there. My heart pounded with fear, certain that the wolf would pick up my scent and devour me. This wasn't any wolf I have ever seen before; it was enormous, ancient-looking, primal. It came closer to where I was crouched, yet it did not find me.

THE TRUTH I KNOW NOW

Jesus hid me from that wolf. He was my refuge in a moment of danger, protecting me in the spirit even when I didn't yet understand. At that time in my life, I believed that animals could appear as "spirit guides." I even bought a book called *Animal Speak* to interpret such dreams. I remember looking up "wolf" the morning after this dream. The passage in the book read: "You're being spiritually and physically protected at all times." I laugh now at the irony. The enemy will always try to imitate and pervert God's truth, twisting it just enough to deceive. But the reality is this: had I stepped out of the gate that wolf would have devoured me. Jesus hid me in the wilderness.

Psalm 27:5 (KJV)
For in the time of trouble He shall hide me in His pavilion; In the secret place of His tabernacle, He shall hide me; He shall set me high upon a rock.

Matthew 10:16

"Look, I'm sending you out like sheep among wolves. Therefore be as shrewd as serpents and as innocent as doves."

Matthew 18:12–14

"If someone has a hundred sheep, and one of them goes astray, won't he leave the ninety-nine on the hillside and go and search for the stray? And if he finds it, truly I tell you, he rejoices over that sheep more than over the ninety-nine that did not go astray. In the same way, it is not the will of your Father in heaven that one of these little ones perish."

Black Magic and Tarot

The following summer, I took a solo trip to California to visit my childhood friend and see the sequoias. While there, I also met up with a woman I had met months earlier at the ancestralization retreat. She was much older than me, but I've always been an old soul, and I told her that whenever I was in California, I would stop by.

I picked her up early one morning, and we went for breakfast at an oceanfront spot she recommended—quaint, low-key, and gorgeous. We drove up and down the coast of Rio, taking in all its beauty. On our way to the restaurant, we passed a crystal shop and decided to circle back afterward. But when we returned, the shop was nowhere to be found. The signage we saw earlier was there, but we couldn't find the shop. It was strange. We circled the area, even took down the number, but the store remained elusive. I thought: *Okay, let's just keep going—if it's this tough to find, it's not for us.* My friend called the number; a woman answered and gave us directions. Even then, it was difficult to locate. The whole ordeal felt unsettling.

When we finally arrived, the shop didn't look anything like we expected. It was closed, and there were no crystals or displays—just a couch, two chairs, and some random décor. As we turned to leave, the woman appeared and caught us before we reached the car. She invited us inside. I was ready to say, "That's okay, we're good," but my friend, being more easygoing, accepted her invitation.

My friend wanted a reading; I had no interest. In spaces like that, I was always very selective—I was sensing something in my spirit, and it wasn't good. I wasn't feeling this woman. As my friend spoke with her about why she wanted a reading, I felt the woman's attention on me, even though she was looking and engaging with my friend. It was eerily uncomfortable. Then she shifted her gaze, looked at me, and asked if I wanted a reading. I said, "No, thank you." She pressed and I thought, *Well, we've taken up this much of her time; I'll just get a palm reading and disengage.* Before I even sat down, she pointed to my bracelet and told me it wasn't tourmaline, as I had thought, but another stone often mistaken for it. Again, very unsettling. Was she trying to hint that I wasn't safe here?

Then she told us that one of us would need to wait outside while the other's reading was done in private. I remember thinking, *Why?* She could stay in for mine—nothing to hide here. My friend went first, and I waited in the car. When it was my turn, I went in, but mentally I put up a spiritual wall. I wasn't interested in what she had to say and was ready to leave. I let her speak, offering no reactions or input.

Still, she grew very detailed about my life—too detailed. Then she said, "You need a chakra cleanse to clear a spiritual block." She led me toward a backroom. As I stepped inside, my heart sank. I had seen this very moment before—in a dream months earlier. The room was identical. It was the warning God had given me. I knew then that I wasn't supposed to be there. I silently prayed for protection, wanting to turn around, but I couldn't. I just prayed for God to cover me.

The Dream of Foresight
(prior to the encounter)

Someone tried to take from me in the spirit. The woman appeared in the form of an old childhood friend I had not trusted from high school. She asked to do Reiki and clear a spiritual block. I remember a voice saying, *No one outside of you can do anything for you: you already know.* As I was hearing this, she started the Reiki: her head was at the level of my navel. She growled and pushed up and said, "Clear her elemental conscious." I felt a force surge from my navel through my upper torso. As it reached my head, I woke up with a gasp.

> **THE TRUTH I KNOW NOW**
>
> 1 John 2:20,27
> But you have an anointing from the Holy One, and all of you know the truth. As for you, the anointing you received from Him remains in you, and you don't need anyone to teach you. Instead, his anointing teaches you about all things and is true and is not a lie; just as it has taught you, remain in Him.

Back to the Store

When I was leaving the shop, the woman was sitting on the couch facing the door. She had given me a rock to take home, and I remember saying goodbye, telling her to take care—and inexplicably, that I loved her. I didn't know why I said the love part at the time. Even when it came out, I thought—*What?* When I looked back at her, her eyes were roaming—they were not her eyes. In that moment, I knew that black magic was performed. I was afraid.

When I got to the car, my friend gave me a box and said, "I got you something from a nearby shop—open it." Inside was a bracelet with a cross charm—it was beautiful. I was shocked; I thought to myself, *You believe in God?* I wondered why she would buy that, of all things. We had never spoken about God, and she didn't know me outside of our connection at the ancestralization retreat. All I know now is that God is good, and his faithful love endures forever. He answered my prayer for covering and He was with me in that moment, protecting me from the hands of the enemy.

A few months had passed since the trip, and I was sharing this experience with two friends who had also attended the indigenous retreat. All I kept hearing from them was, "Get that rock out of your house—now!" I didn't waste a second more. I wrapped the rock up, drove to the closest river, and smashed it with a hammer. The sound was inexplicable—it gave me chills. I threw the pieces off a bridge into the water.

THE TRUTH I KNOW NOW

I was in the enemy's territory. She was a high-ranking agent of darkness, and when you operate outside of God's covenant, you become fair game. Even in that moment, God never left me. I prayed for protection, and He responded when my friend placed that cross in my hand. I didn't understand it then, but God did—and His faithful love endures forever.

Deuteronomy 7:26
Do not bring any detestable thing into your house, or you will be set apart for destruction like it.

Leviticus 19:31
Do not turn to mediums or consult spiritists, or you will be defiled by them; I am the LORD your God.

Ephesians 6:10–12
Finally, be strengthened by the LORD and by his vast strength. Put on the full armor of God so that you can stand against the schemes of the devil. For we do not wrestle against flesh and blood, but against principalities, against powers, against the rulers of the darkness of this age, against spiritual hosts of wickedness in the heavenly places.

DREAM: TAROT

In this dream, a woman asked me if I knew how to read tarot. I replied, "Not for others, just something I occasionally do for myself." She insisted, saying, "You need to read to people."

THE TRUTH I KNOW NOW

She was an agent of darkness, a spiritual attack from the enemy. It is important to discern spirit—whether in dreams, visions, or the physical—in order to see who is speaking to you. God says to test every spirit. The gifts He has given me were never meant to be used in the kingdom of darkness. God is not in tarot cards, nor are His plans for your life revealed through them.

1 John 4:1
Dear friends, do not believe every spirit, but test the spirits to see if they are from God, because many false prophets have gone out into the world.

Jeremiah 29:11–13 (NIV)
"For I know the plans I have for you," declares the LORD, "plans to prosper you and not to harm you, plans to give you hope and a future. Then you will call on me and come and pray to me, and I will listen to you. You will seek me and find me when you seek me with all your heart."

When you open your spirit to such readings, you open yourself to deception and come into agreement with lies. These practices separate you from God. They open doors, giving permission for any kind of spirit to enter our lives. These are departed spirits and demons masquerading as light. These unholy and unclean spirits use divination to manipulate, deceive, and mix truth with lies: an entanglement pulling you further from God and delaying your destiny—His will for your life. Your time and life are too precious to risk. Stay in step with the LORD; He will never lead you astray.

Divinations: The Illusion of Clarity

I wrestled with whether to share these experiences. Much of what I've written in these chapters was hard to revisit, but this part was especially difficult to release into the world. I resisted, and felt vulnerable, but I trust in God's plan. My discomfort is no match for the lives and souls it may protect from wandering down the wrong path, or for the hope it may bring to those finding their way back home. The need for people to hear and know the truth—to be able to recognize the many schemes and tricks of the enemy—surpasses all. This is to help in awakening a generation that has fallen into a deep slumber. No matter how positive, innocent, or even "truthful" these practices may appear, beneath them lies deception. The enemy is cunning, weaving lies with just enough truth to sound convincing—ever so strategically. And for those who are not rooted in the Word of God, as I once was, the deception can slip in unnoticed, bypassing every radar.

Now that my foundation is anchored in Jesus Christ, I can clearly see the lies I once missed. It has taught me how vital it is to know God's Word, for we do not live on bread alone. Looking back, I see all the places where I was weak in Scripture: the very gaps in truth that became open doors for the enemy's influence. Those openings gave the adversary leverage, and in my immaturity, he tried to destroy me. But God's Word never returns void.

He has given us both His Word and His Spirit as a compass. I now understand the importance of putting on the full armor of God and standing firm in His truth. As I read through my old writings and listened back to those recordings, part of me wished I had been then who I am now in Christ. The conversations would have gone very differently. But I also know that pain is never wasted. What the enemy intended for harm; God has turned for good.

Matthew 4:4
"It is written: Man must not live on bread alone but on every word that comes from the mouth of God."

Romans 8:28
We know that all things work together for the good of those who love God, who are called according to his purpose.

Genesis 50:20
You planned evil against me; God planned it for good to bring about the present result: the survival of many people.

Before sharing this part of my journey, let's be crystal clear on what God says about divinations and anything of the like.

Deuteronomy 18:10–12
No one among you is to sacrifice his son or daughter in the fire, practice divination, tell fortunes, interpret omens, practice sorcery, cast spells, consult a medium or a spiritist, or inquire of the dead. Everyone who does these acts is detestable to

the LORD, *and the* LORD *your God is driving out the nations before you because of these detestable acts.*

Cowry Shell Divination #1

In Dagara cosmology, a cowry shell divination is considered a traditional spiritual practice used to gain insight, guidance, and healing. It is performed by a diviner who claims to communicate with ancestral spirits and elemental beings. As I noted earlier, the shells are believed to carry messages from the spirit realm regarding personal issues, community matters, and spiritual alignment with the physical. The shells are cast, along with other objects, onto a designated surface and then interpreted based on their positions, relationships, and patterns.

The diviner spoke these words to me:

Your gifts and your destiny are so intertwined with ancestral wisdom and knowledge that there is no escaping it. You look familiar—the oracle field that you are beaming is familiar—and your ancestral roots are of such depths that no matter where you are in the world you have no way around this. Better consciously than unconsciously.

This is a very powerful symbol. What is coming is big— so big it will be like your life up to now hasn't even started.

There is growing expectation from your ancestors. Feels like a long time ago you devoted a whole lifetime caring for a whole village or community. And although exhausted at the end of your earthly life, you felt that once you recovered, you would return in order to finish what you left undone—you had a few things to wrap up. When you enter this world, it took time for this memory to push through.

You are like a precious metal, dug out from the depths of earth or the depths of time, brought to the now—cleanse and purify it.

There is a part of you that knows devotion and dedication—a part of you that is disciplined and trustworthy. When you say yes, it means yes. When you say no, it means no. These are things that matter.

A race against time to a future that is full of beauty and colorfulness.

Freshen up your relationship with water—you have been bruised.

There is a water ritual offering to be done—an oath to change and to become an agent of change. This is done around full moon cycles.

Growing like a mountain into visibility. It's not a defiance against anything else; it's just acknowledging who you are. You are an expression of a legacy that is meant to be expressed in this time.

THE TRUTH I KNOW NOW

Stepping outside of God's covenant is an act of defiance—it is seeking guidance apart from Him. The LORD reminds us: "My grace is sufficient for thee: for my strength is made perfect in weakness."

> **1 Samuel 15:23**
> For rebellion is like the sin of divination, and defiance is like wickedness and idolatry. Because you have rejected the word of the LORD.
>
> **Deuteronomy 6:13**
> Fear the LORD your God, worship him, and take your oaths in his name. Do not follow other gods, the gods of the peoples around you.
>
> **Deuteronomy 4:19**
> When you look to the heavens and see the sun, moon, and stars—all the stars in the sky—do not be led astray to bow in worship to them and serve them.

Back to the Divination

Your light is so bright, so powerful; it is not subject to further dissection or understanding—it is taken as is. Something that is sweet needs no further debate.

The devoted part of you is an extension of your spiritual acumen: you will cross paths with many people, and your radiance is enough for them to feel transformed. This is an ancient wisdom.

Your osirah is quite regal—very regal. Somehow this is inspired by an energy that is an expression of the legacy that you represent. Where do you trace your family line?

Whoa, whoa: you are in touch with something so big.

What you carry is a thing that is so essential to the healing of the family at large. You have to embrace it, it's inevitable.

End of Divination

When someone—whether knowingly or unconsciously being used by the enemy—tries to conceal information or cloak their words, it's often an indicator that the truth would reveal harm or error. If it were laid out plainly, most people would never agree to it. He mentioned "my light" and how it's so powerful as if it is my own. The light that we carry is only through Jesus Christ—He is the light of the world. We are merely representations of His light and of the Kingdom of God. The beauty in following Jesus Christ is that He never has to hide or disguise Himself. He doesn't manipulate or mask His intentions. With Him, it is simply yes or no, truth without deception—*you can take it or leave it.*

Joshua 24:15 (NIV)
But if serving the Lord seems undesirable to you, then choose for yourselves this day whom you will serve, whether the gods your ancestors served beyond the Euphrates, or the gods of the Amorites, in whose land you are living. But as for me and my household, we will serve the Lord.

Now, let's look back at this portion of the divination: "There is a water ritual offering to be done being an oath to change and to become an agent of change. This is done around full moon cycles." If it had been spoken plainly, some could even call it layman's terms, it would sound more like this: "Hey, by the way—you'll need to take an oath to change from who you are today and become an agent that goes against God's will. And you'll need to make this oath in worship to the moon."

That sounds different, right? Most people would pause and ponder the second version. The enemy and his minions would probably not get many people on their team using the latter line. The enemy has to hide and mask his true identity and agenda in order to recruit. He hides his motives until it's too late, until he has you where he wants you—bound.

This is not a new tactic. Scripture shows us exactly where this strategy has played out. Let's take a look at when Satan tempted Jesus on the mountain after Jesus had fasted forty days—he too was in a vulnerable state.

Matthew 4:3–11

*Then the tempter approached him and said, "If you are the Son of God, tell these stones to become bread." He answered, "It is written: 'Man must not live on bread alone but on every word that comes from the mouth of God.'" Then the devil took him to the holy city, had him stand on the pinnacle of the temple, and said to him, "If you are the Son of God, throw yourself down. For it is written: 'He will give his angels orders concerning you, and they will support you with their hands so that you will not strike your foot against a stone.'" Jesus told him, "It is also written: 'Do not test the L*ORD *your God.'" Again, the devil took him to a very high mountain and* *showed him all the kingdoms of the world and their splendor. And he said to him, "I will give you all these things if you will fall down and worship me." Then Jesus told him, "Go away, satan! For it is written: 'Worship the L*ord *your God, and serve only him.'"*

I wish my response had been like Jesus's during that time in my life. So, you might ask—what was I missing? The most important thing: I went into battle without my sword. I didn't know Scripture; I wasn't rooted in the Word of God. Jesus didn't fight Satan using His own logic, nor did he defeat him with physical strength—he didn't punch him in the face. He spoke the Word of God.

Ephesians 6:11,17
Put on the full armor of God so that you can stand against the schemes of the devil. Take the helmet of salvation and the sword of the Spirit—which is the word of God.

Another example of this is Eve and the Serpent in the Garden of Eden:

Genesis 3:1–6
*Now the serpent was the most cunning of all the wild animals that the L*ord *God had made. He said to the woman, "Did God really say, 'You can't eat from any tree in the garden'?" The woman said to the serpent: "We may eat the fruit from the trees in the garden. But not the fruit of the tree in the middle*

of the garden, God said, 'You must not eat it or touch it, or you will die.'" "No! You will certainly not die," the serpent said to the woman. "In fact, God knows that when you eat it your eyes will be opened and you will be like God, knowing good and evil." The woman saw that the tree was good for food and delightful to look at, and that it was desirable for obtaining wisdom. So, she took some of its fruit and ate it.

Unfortunately, my temptation played out more like Eve's in the garden. Thank God for His mercy, love, and grace. Let's not take it for granted. I don't take it lightly, especially after the valley I experienced; there is nowhere I would rather be than with my Creator. We can apply these lessons directly to our lives. Nothing has changed but the time—the enemy still uses the same methods of deceit. The form of deceit you'll see throughout my journey, and one of the most dangerous forms, is equivocation. It is the use of ambiguous or misleading language to obscure the truth or to avoid committing to a clear stance. It may not sound like an outright lie, but it carries the same deadly intent.

We see it in business, in leadership, even in everyday conversations—language crafted to mislead the masses. But God warns us: test every *spirit*. Now let's take a closer look at the serpent's interaction with Eve in the Garden. Let's focus on spotting the equivocation, the subtle omissions, and the half-truths designed to conceal what was really at stake by simply omitting important information.

Where the serpent says, "No! You will certainly not die," we see equivocal language at work. The serpent was being deceptive by withholding information. What he was really saying to Eve is that she would not physically experience death if she ate from the forbidden tree. What he concealed was a deeper truth: she would suffer spiritual death, separation from God, and exile from the Garden of Eden.

And of course, his deceit didn't just affect Eve—it set into motion consequences for all of humanity. As Solomon reminds us in Scripture, "there is nothing new under the sun." It's true. The enemy still strikes where we are most vulnerable—our blind spots, our unhealed wounds, our old traumas, all forms of weakness. But what does God say: "My Grace is sufficient for thee: for my strength is made perfect in weakness."

Cowry Shell Divination #2

Before the divination began, I shared with him that I was feeling the need to protect myself. I wanted clarity on what "my medicine" was—a term they used that could be compared to "gift(s)." Remember, the enemy isn't creative; he mimics. I also wanted to understand why so many animals were showing up around me. The night before this divination session, I had dreamt vividly of the number *40* and a *triangle*—both crystal clear. At the time, I turned to a search engine for answers. Searching what it meant "spiritually," I found interpretations that it was an angel number telling me I was well protected and loved.

THE TRUTH I KNOW NOW

Scripture paints a much clearer picture. Biblically, the number 40 carries deep significance, representing a season of testing, preparation, or judgment. While the Bible does not explicitly mention the triangle, its three points naturally point to the Trinity: Father, Son, and Holy Spirit. Consider the weight of *40* throughout God's Word:

- **Noah and the Ark**—40 days and 40 nights of rain.
- **Moses and the Israelites**—40 years wandering in the desert before entering the promised land.
- **The Spies in Canaan**—40 days exploring the land.
- **Israel's Captivity**—Delivered into the hands of the Philistines for 40 years.
- **Jesus in the Wilderness**—40 days and 40 nights of fasting before being tempted by Satan.
- **Nineveh**—Given 40 days to repent through Jonah's message.

This *40* was significant. It was not just a number, and it certainly wasn't what the search engine suggested. It was a marker of God's process—His refining fire, His call to repentance before going deeper, and His preparation for greater things to come.

The Divination

You also need to pay attention to wedamé *by bringing them the nourishment that show that you are aware of their presence in your life. Simply means bringing food to nature and spreading it out for the nature beings to consume. That would strengthen and deepen the relationship.*

You have medicine that you are now aware of: otherwise the beings would not be there.

There is ancestral wisdom and power that you are meant to bring into this world. The way you are being called to do your work is more like a flow. You are being invited to go in a seamless fashion. You owe yourself gentleness: the changes are not old enough in you to be considered anchored.

Your medicine is healing and the little people, the kontumblé, *are speaking of the healer in you. You are yet to take office. There are plans that need to be implemented first.*

Water and earth are saying you are cleansing the being that you are. Your heart is in a frequency of love and caring. Something magical is happening in your life, your brilliance will show as an expression of being in touch with the ancient ancestors.

Something has to be done with the kontumblé *at the center of nature who raves about the healer in you. Saying they are fully a part of it, that they are your counselor, your guide, your initiator of all the initiations you have to do in order to rise dignifiedly and elegantly in this work. This model is going to be wrapped elementally:*

multi-facedness you are bringing to community you will not be repeating something verbatim, but it will be unique, and it will bear your signature. You have ancient wisdom that you came into this world with. This relationship has to be energized.

Pause

THE TRUTH I KNOW NOW

John 14:26
"The Counselor, the Holy Spirit, whom the Father will send in my name, will teach you all things and remind you of everything I have told you."

Back to the Divination

There is an intuition and instinct inside of you that is waiting to be activated at the highest level in order to give you a clear sense of direction that is supported by trust.

The path that you are following, the path you have taken is really not treacherous, not hiding some traps in there. Just know this experience put you in a contemplative state and it is in that frequency that you are able to discern what works for you and was doesn't work for you.

The best protection for you comes from this kind of consciousness, the consciousness that allows you to discern what is good and not good.

You don't just take notice, you take action; that is very important. A woman of medicine is not sitting still in contemplation like meditation.

You are in a transitional state, you have crossed into the larger part of who you are. Which is larger than life which is now ready to be invested in contributing in your own way, the way you feel is suitable.

Being able to surround yourself with enough beauty, fullness, and beautiful things so that your whole concentration be on the work that you are called to do. This is a fair trade in the context because operating from a deficit it just not good looking. Anyway, this is not a time of sacrifice, it's a time of devotion, militancy, and to be an instrument of this grand healing scheme.

THE TRUTH I KNOW NOW

The part the enemy never mentions is that this so-called "fair trade" is for your *soul*. And what does it profit a man to gain the whole world, yet in the end lose his soul? A truth that was told during this session—it is for sure a grand healing *scheme*. Only God Almighty heals. Notice how strategically the "trade" was placed in that reading. That's how deception works. Here's the reality: the people who seem to live luxuriously and appear to have it all together—without God Almighty, they are the poorest souls you'll ever encounter. Empty shells. Meanwhile, the one who looks like they're operating from a deficit is often the richest in Christ. Don't be fooled by what society feeds you. Don't drink the Kool-Aid. I've been there, done that. I'll save you the time and warfare.

A life without God only breeds the rat race so many of us are trapped in—isolated, striving, competing, envying our brothers and sisters. This way of life keeps the vicious system alive. People feed into the very thing that oppresses them. But you were made for more than that. What happened to building each other up and truly caring for one another? We are so much stronger together.

Psalm 46:10 (KJV)
Be still and know that I am GOD.

Psalm 1:1–2
Blessed is the one who does not walk in the advice of the wicked or stand in the pathway with sinners or sit in the company of mockers. Instead, his delight is in the Lord's instruction, and he meditates on it day and night.

1 Thessalonians 5:12–15
Now we ask you, brothers and sisters, to give recognition to those who labor among you and lead you in the Lord and admonish you, and to regard them very highly in love because of their work. Be at peace among yourselves. And we exhort you, brothers and

sisters: warn those who are idle, comfort the discouraged, help the weak, be patient with everyone. See to it that no one repays evil for evil to anyone, but always pursue what is good for one another and for all.

Back to the Divination

Formalize your relationship with kontumblé *to give yourself an added resource. Refuse to censor yourself, your feelings, your desires, your aspiration. Because you cannot afford at this level of your growth to deny yourself something, you have to allow and give permission to yourself to want something, to aspire for something, even if it is not spoken. It should still be considered valid.*

And this is the way you can therefore arrive at a place where you have a way of proving you didn't deny yourself anything, no feeling of suppression.

THE TRUTH I KNOW NOW

First, I have to say—it hurt to listen to that last part again. I can't believe that would slip under anyone's radar—something so juvenile in nature. I wonder how old the spirit was that spoke this. You *must* deny yourself many things in this world for your good and the good of all—it's called growing up. Could you imagine what the world would be like if we all believed this? Chaos. Self-indulgence. A society ruled by desire rather than discipline.

James 1:14–15
Each person is tempted when he is drawn away and enticed by his own evil desire. Then after desire has conceived it gives birth to sin, and when sin is fully grown, it gives birth to death.

Luke 9:23
Then he said to them all, "If anyone wants to follow after me, let him deny himself, take up his cross daily, and follow me."

2 Timothy 3:1–5
But know this: Hard times will come in the last days. For people will be lovers of self, lovers of money, boastful, proud, demeaning, disobedient to parents, ungrateful, unholy, unloving, irreconcilable, slanderers, without self-control, brutal, without love for what is good, traitors, reckless, conceited, lovers of pleasure rather than lovers of God, holding to the form of godliness but denying its power. Have nothing to do with such people.

1 Thessalonians 5:5–8
You are all children of light and children of the day. We do not belong to the night or to the darkness. So

then, let us not be like others, who are asleep, but let us stay awake and be self-controlled. For those who sleep, sleep at night, and those who get drunk, get drunk at night. But since we belong to the day, let us be self-controlled, putting on faith and love as a breastplate, and the hope of salvation as a helmet.

Back to the Divination

You have this duality in you I don't know how to say that— you are a woman of two faces, two feet, maybe four feet—a combination of cultures and tradition that you are called to synthesize to make whole. This is a unique position to be in: your bones should be rattling with energy from all these places, place of origin to give you access to this unique self-positioning in the global context. That's who you are and what you commit yourself to be while walking this dimension.

End of Divination

THE TRUTH I KNOW NOW

I struggled to get this out. The enemy attacked me on so many levels, hoping I would stay silent and not expose these practices. But God reigns on the throne. I serve a mighty God—a living God, Alpha and Omega, Beginning and the

End, the great I AM. And in Jesus Christ, we have authority over every power of darkness.

Make no mistake: in these practices you are not talking to your loved ones or anything holy: you are speaking to unclean, evil spirits. Call them whatever you want, dress them up with different names, but they all lead to the same destruction. As much as people may want to believe they're connecting with a loved one or receiving help from a benevolent force, the truth is sobering: they are opening themselves to demons, departed spirits, and forces of darkness. And worse, they're handing over first-class access to the most intimate details of their lives.

Here's the difference: God is all-knowing and all-seeing, Satan is not. He relies on his minions and agents to collect information about you. Participating in these practices is like leaving the keys in the front door of your home—an open invitation for the thief to walk right in.

Ephesians 1:20–23

He exercised this power in Christ by raising him from the dead and seating him at the right hand in the heavens: far above every ruler and authority, power and dominion, and every title given, not only in this age but also in the one to come. And he subjected everything under his feet and appointed him as head over everything in the church, which is his body, the fullness of the one who fills all things in every way.

> **Isaiah 43:12–13**
> I alone declared, saved, and proclaimed: and not some foreign god among you. I am He alone, and none can rescue from my power. I act, and who can reverse it?

Kontumblé Divination

I met this diviner at the elemental retreat. She was known for her connection to the *kontumblé*. In West African tradition, the *kontumblé* are said to be highly intelligent, small beings—playful and compassionate, often compared to fairies and elves in other cultures. After my second divination with the spiritual teacher, where the *kontumblé* had come up in both sessions, I reached a point where I wanted to understand their supposed "role" in my life. So I reached out to her. I shared with her a portion of my previous divination—the one performed by the spiritual teacher that focused on the *kontumblé*.

This is what he had spoken to me during that divination:

Something has to be done with the kontumblé *who are raving about the healer in you. They are fully a part of it. They are your counsel, your guide, the initiator of all the initiates you have to do in order to rise with dignity and elegantly in this work.*

She listened carefully and then began her own divination. She explained that the *kontumblé* were "happy to hear I was next" and that they required extra liquor as an offering on my behalf. She went on to describe the spirits that were present for this divination and those that were around me: *wedamé* (said to appear as an animal of protection), the Archangel Michael ("very heavy with you"), and "there is another angel that's with you—not sure of the name, I just see GDL."

Then she said the words that made my spirit tighten: "The *kontumblé* were ready to speak."

They said:

- *Go where the shore meets the water: where the shore meets the water.*
- *Important for you to contemplate where the shore meets the water and learn about the starfish. Study them, how they move, eat, live, their ecosystem: this will bring you closer to us. Also, the stars in the sky.*
- *Do you remember the water ritual during the Elemental Immersion indigenous retreat? The underwater city, heart of the earth: the veins of the earth.*

The third bullet gave me chills. I wasn't afraid—but it shook something deep inside me. I knew the detail in what I had seen during the water ritual at the Elemental Immersion retreat, and she did not. As I shared earlier in this book, when I dipped under the water for the third time, it was no longer the lake bottom that met my eyes. I saw something else—what I could only describe as tunnels. Many of them. Surrounding me. It was not the lake bottom that I had seen in the first two dips.

- *Find the caves, go deep into the caves. From home, from room and shore where the water meets. When you hit a wall just make a turn.*
- *Mermaids, connection with earth is very much with water and ocean. And how water is different. Guidance in the cave.*
- *Journey there with intention creating the space. Activating magic. Meet the* kontumblé *acknowledging there is a difference by going there physically and being in your room.*
- *Bring food. Cave or cave-like dwelling.*
- *You are spirit, you cannot be disconnected.* [This was in response to me saying I felt disconnected from spirit.]
- *You need the journey.*
- *Mountain: make a mineral shrine trust images and activation. Tell the ancestors give them the details. Mountain shrine giving structure to this new beginning so that you are more grounded and have a sense of direction.*
- *Water shrine to carry you to* kontumblé.
- *The water ritual at the retreat was barely scratching the surface: will relate to several lifetimes.*

End of Divination

The weekend after getting this divination I went to the ocean with my husband. I sat on a cluster of rocks right on the shoreline—where the water meets the land. I had no clue what to do there. I found a book on starfish; when I finished it, I wasn't sure why I needed to know any of it, other than maybe to one day share some fun starfish facts with children.

As I closed the book, I noticed a young man walking along the shoreline. It was a hot day, yet he was fully dressed, wearing sneakers and a backpack. I watched as he approached the water, only to back away quickly each time, as if afraid to get wet—almost childlike. This annoyed me a bit; I felt him to be a distraction. As he passed by me, he continued to walk down the shoreline continuing this behavior. I looked around and no one was with him. The further away he got, I realized he had some sort of disability. In that instant I felt horrible—shame washed over me. How quickly I had judged him. I had been so self-absorbed, yet I had the opportunity in that moment to offer that young man a kind word, a smile, inspiration, some of my snacks, a hello … anything. Instead, I sat there consumed in my own nonsense. As he grew smaller in the distance, I wrestled inside—surely, I could catch up to him, but what would I say? By the time I made up my mind, he was halfway down the beach. I looked around again for his parents or a chaperone and there was no one in sight.

Then it hit me: Was that it? Was this the encounter the *kontumblé* spoke of? Was this the "test," the lesson, the measure of my heart? If so, I had failed.

A few months later, I stopped by our local arboretum to see the new foliage and clear my mind. I sat on a bench beneath one of my favorite cedar trees, finishing up a book I was reading. I heard children nearby, a large group of some sort. Looking up,

I saw a little girl running toward me. She was autistic, unable to speak, but vocal in her own way. Her arms were wide open, her smile radiant. I didn't know what to do other than hug her and give her just as much love as she was running to give me. Instinctively, I opened my arms to her. Before I knew it, she was in my embrace. Her chaperone, rushing after her, arrived too late and apologized profusely. I told him no apology was needed. But when he gently pulled her away, she let out the loudest cry I've ever heard. I wasn't sure what was happening, but I felt it was spiritual for sure. Unlike before, this time I was grateful. Grateful that my arms had been open. Grateful that I did not miss it.

THE TRUTH I KNOW NOW

These experiences only pressed me closer to the truth: and to know we are only scratching the surface when it comes to what we know in this world and who truly is in control. It wasn't until deeper into my walk with God that the Holy Spirit revealed the meaning of the phrase spoken to me during this divination: "where the shore meets the water." Revelation 10 describes a vision involving a mighty angel holding a scroll, setting his right foot on the sea and his left foot on the land. During this divination, it was said: "It is important for you to contemplate, where the shore meets the water."

> **Revelation 10:5–7**
> Then the angel that I had seen standing on the sea and on the land raised his right hand to heaven. He swore by the one who lives forever and ever, who created heaven and what is in it, the earth and what is in it, and the sea and what is in it, "There will no longer be a delay, but in the days when the seventh angel will blow his trumpet, then the mystery of God will be completed, as he announced to his servants the prophets."

God's Word in Revelation 10 provides the full context for what that means. In reading the full chapter important points where highlighted: the *little book* that John is instructed to consume, showing that God's words can be both sweet and bitter to the prophet when proclaiming God's truth during the time of judgment, and it being the time to receive, internalize, and proclaim the Word of God. The declaration of "delay no longer" points to God's will and purposes being fulfilled, and that there will be no further delay in God's plan for the end times.

This was a warning in so many ways. I was standing between two worlds, two kingdoms. And there will be no extra time given for anyone. God doesn't have favorites; I had a choice. It was important for me to contemplate which path I would choose. Without God's Word, I would not stand a chance. I sat in stillness with this revelation, determined to never again be out of alignment with the LORD.

2 Peter 3:9–10
The LORD does not delay his promise as some understand delay, but is patient with you, not wanting any to perish but all to come to repentance. But the day of the Lord will come like a thief. The heavens will disappear with a roar; the elements will be destroyed by fire, and the earth and everything done in it will be laid bare.

Deuteronomy 4:19
When you look to the heavens and see the sun, moon, and stars—all the stars in the sky—do not be led astray to bow in worship to them and serve them.

Matthew 4:8–11
Again, the devil took him to a very high mountain and showed him all the kingdoms of the world and their splendor. And he said to him, "I will give you all these things if you will fall down and worship me." Then Jesus told him, "Go away, satan! For it is written: 'Worship the LORD your God, and serve only him.'"

I shared the passage in Matthew to highlight that there are many kingdoms in this world. When you operate outside of God's Kingdom, you place yourself on a path of destruction. For we do not fight against flesh and blood.

I have heard *kontumblé* speak through people. It is unlike anything I can fully describe—it is otherworldly. Yet even through these encounters, I was never afraid. They pushed me to keep seeking the truth—what these beings were, how the unseen overlap, and whether they truly had influence over our lives. What I can testify is this: I've seen enough to run for God and never look back. Yes, these spirits, unclean and evil, are real. And yes, if you grant them access, they will wreak havoc and chaos in your life. Maybe not immediately—but inevitably. There is no light in them. They cannot give peace, freedom, or life. And the cost they demand is one no soul can afford to pay.

These divinations are ambiguous, a mixture of truth and deception. With God there is no pretense. God's truth remains unshakable.

John 14:26
"But the Counselor, the Holy Spirit, whom the Father will send in my name, will teach you all things and remind you of everything I have told you."

Robin and the Power Animal Retrieval

Around this time, I came across a book on animal communication. I had begun entertaining the idea that animals could also serve as spiritual guides—helpers on our journey who carried messages and insight. Looking back now, it sounds funny—I'm laughing as I write this. But this is how deeply I had committed to seeking truth—I was deep in the rabbit hole.

There had been an influx of animal encounters, as though they were gravitating to me for something. Every day something new in nature became more alive; things were happening that I couldn't explain. That morning, I had a call scheduled with the author of the book I was reading, a woman named Mary, to learn more about shamanic journeying and connecting with spirit animals.

About an hour before the call, a robin appeared at my kitchen window. It didn't just perch on the windowsill, it flew up and pecked at the glass repeatedly—over and over again. The robin continued for nearly two hours, throughout the call and even afterward. This has never happened before. Laughing to myself, I recorded it and thought: *The robin must know I'm speaking with Mary today.* Mary and I spoke for about an hour. The conversation was energetic, fluid, and felt authentic. I asked her to perform the "power animal retrieval" she wrote about in her book. She agreed and told me she would send it once it was completed.

A few days later, I received my session recording of what Mary channeled. She said she traveled her usual path into the "lower world," down through the tunnel, and before she could see anything else, she described the robin—dancing and hoping before her:

> *"Robin's message: I want to help her find the best morsels." Robins eat worms and bugs on the ground in search for the best morsels. "You have a beautiful song inside you so do whatever it takes to share it with the world."*
>
> *Call on the robin when you've experienced a surprising and profound spiritual revelation or awakening. You're a happy person and your joy affects others in a positive way. You have a past life connection to Christ, whether you're Christian or not and you know that you are on a divine mission in life. You're a dedicated spiritual seeker, using as many resources as possible to continue evolving as a spiritual being. You like to be settled in one place more so than moving around a lot. Your primary assignment while you're on the planet is, to the best of your ability, to express the will of God in all you do and all you say.*

Side Note

She had me right here. Up to this point, I was blown away—it was so precise. I was ready to talk to animals. But remember this: there will always be a misstep, something your spirit will catch if you're truly listening.

Back to the Divination

Koi fish message: Are you here to help Brittany? "Absolutely!" What are you bringing to Brittany? "Prosperity and abundance: Courage, strength, and determination. Nonconformity and perseverance."

Third animal's message: I could sense a third animal around that is very connected to you, but he is very shy and he would not reveal himself to me and he said that when you learn to journey and work with your power animals that you are supposed to go and ask who is this power animal that is so shy but has a lot of meaning in your life. All he would tell me is that he is going to help you do your searching for spirituality and the meaning, your mission in this life.

End of Divination

THE TRUTH I KNOW NOW

Even in those places, God never left me. At the time, I wasn't walking with Him as I am now, so I couldn't fully appreciate the moments where Christ broke through. Looking back, I celebrate and smile because Jesus kept shining through every place I went.

Although this experience was beautiful, even describing my nature and personality—I don't leave any door open for the enemy to deceive. Divination in any form is not the way of God. And that third animal hiding was just creepy. Let's be honest—likely a ploy of the enemy to lure me further into believing that I need anything outside of God for guidance, pulling me deeper into this pit. God provides all. There is nothing we need from any animal spirit. God created man in His image and gave us dominion over the fish of the sea, the birds of the sky, and every creature that crawls on the earth.

Deuteronomy 4:15–18
Diligently watch yourselves—because you did not see any form on the day the LORD spoke to you out of the fire at Horeb—so you don't act corruptly and make an idol for yourselves in the shape of any figure: a male or female form, or the form of any animal on the earth, any winged creature that flies in the sky, any creature that crawls on the ground, or any fish in the waters under the earth.

2 Corinthians 11:3–4
But I fear that as the serpent deceived Eve by his cunning, your minds may be seduced from a sincere and pure devotion to Christ. For if a person comes and preaches another Jesus, whom we did not preach, or you receive a different spirit, which you had not received, or a different gospel, which you had not accepted, you put up with it splendidly!

The danger in these practices is how harmless they appear. They're dressed in innocence, leading people to believe there's no risk. The enemy is crafty. Scripture tells us we must test every spirit: be as shrewd as serpents and innocent as doves. Satan is the master of deceit, father of lies, an imitator of light, and perverter of the Word.

Matthew 10:16
"Look, I'm sending you out like sheep among wolves. Therefore, be as shrewd as serpents and as innocent as doves."

Water Divination

Water divination is another spiritual practice within Dagara cosmology. It is believed to provide insight, diagnose issues, guide decisions, and bring healing. Diviners interpret the water's reflective surface to receive messages from the spiritual realm. This particular divination was given by one of the support staff I met during the retreat, who had trained under the same spiritual teacher. He began by saying:

This is related to the other world. You have healing hands. The first thing I saw was the light of your hands and how it can be used for healing: the right hand specifically.

Hertz, they want you to listen to this sound frequency before bed. This opens certain meridian points and chakra points in your body.

Pause

> **THE TRUTH I KNOW NOW**
>
> There is power in sound frequency and the music we listen to. Sounds and frequencies can dismantle or invite energy—dispel or attract spirits. Protect your gates.
>
> > 1 Samuel 16:23
> > Whenever the evil spirit came on Saul, David would pick up his lyre and play, and Saul would then be relieved, feel better, and the evil spirit would leave him.

Back to the Divination

The picture that I'm seeing is of you in the kitchen and you're cutting onions, you're cooking and your cutting onions. You're by the sink and you're looking outwards and as you're cutting the onion a picture jogs into your mind about your father, and I'm seeing back to when you were little when you were a child.

The image I am seeing is you as a child and your father holding your hand and he's walking you through life and he's showing you things—he's been a constant guardian support but it's time to transition from this relationship—he's always held your hand and has been your source of comfort. What I'm seeing is your relationship with your father has always been one of comfort, one of protection and one of sheltering and that sheltering has always put that blanket of comfortability around you to where you have been scared to go out to explore the world and explore things and even explore your own spirituality from what I'm seeing here. This is a hindrance to certain things in your life that need to happen and how you need to move forward. Because you're still Daddy's little girl: you're still that little girl that is holding on to his hand. You have to let his hand go.

The little girl in you is still holding dominant to the clinging of the Father. And what I'm seeing is very clear. You'll have to do a lot of work around this especially your little girl and her fear that your father has always shielded, protected and has not really exposed you to the world. And you carried that to adulthood. Even in your relationships now, but what you don't realize is that you're not allowing others to love you fully, especially men in your relationships: they're competing with Dad. You won't be able to move forward until you change this pattern. It was necessary in your early age, but the dynamic has to change. So, you have to start journeying on your own inner power and your own work, figuring out and learning about your medicine and now rely on the power of yourself and your ancestors and the beings from the other world and other side. You're Dad has done his role, he's done his job; you have to give him a break.

Pause

THE TRUTH I KNOW NOW

I found this both unsettling and illuminating—how these unclean, departed spirits monitor and study you. They are not omnipresent, but they are cunning enough to plant a thought meant to bait you. It's your choice whether to entertain it, whether to bite. I would often find myself contemplating exactly how he described, gazing out the kitchen window and that has always been the nature of my relationship with my father—one that will not change. I sat frozen as he spoke. It felt intrusive, yet they have no access to what has not been legally given. Everything he said was to encourage me to move away from my Fathers—both physical and heavenly. To move away from what has covered me in both the physical and spiritual. What's interesting is that it wasn't only about moving away from my Fathers covering, but also about replacing them and learning to 'rely' on another source or power outside of them. Remember this: if God is not your Source, then you are drawing from another power and force—it is not your own, and it is not free. As I was writing this section, I left a placeholder to come back with Scripture. The phrase I heard in my spirit was "without Me you can do nothing." When I searched for these words, John 15:5 came up—*yes, that's it*. At first, I didn't realize the connection, but then something beautiful happened: my father, who sends Scripture every morning to our family group chat, also sends me a direct message. That very morning, he sent me a GIF with John 15:5 on it. God is so good—and His Word is living!

> **John 15:5**
> "I am the vine; you are the branches. The one who remains in me and I in him produces much fruit, because you can do nothing without me."

This reading had been very much physical and spiritual. Looking back as I document these times, God has shown me where He was with me all along. He never left me, even in those places. This particular moment not only brought me to tears but also to a deep stillness. It reminded me how much He is in the details of our lives—and how deeply our Father loves us. Reading it back, while writing this book, I see the symbolism of both my earthly father and my heavenly Father.

My physical father on earth has always protected and sheltered me. We have always shared a spiritual connection, like in moments such as this that bring confirmation from the Spirit into the physical. Another moment, far more profound, became one of the core reasons for my belief in God from childhood. During my senior year of high school, I found myself in an abusive relationship. One day, as I was being harmed, I silently prayed: *God, if You are real, help me.* Before the last word was out, there was a knock at the door. It was my father. I heard his voice asking if I was there, and I couldn't believe what was happening. How did he know where I was? It felt surreal.

The car ride home, in the truck, was silent—no words were spoken. He had no idea I was being harmed. He only knew that I wasn't where I was supposed to be and he was upset. I had told my parents that I'd be at my best friend's house. But the only thought that was louder than anything else was: *God is real. He sees me. He hears me.* When we got home, my Mom was in the living room causally watching a show; I thought for sure I was going to hear it from her. I braced myself for the lecture—and nothing. I asked her why Dad had come for me and how he knew where I was. Still in disbelief, I listened as she told me: "I don't know. He jumped up from sleep—he barely got his pants on before he ran out the door. I asked where he was going and he just said, 'I'm going to get my daughter.'"

To this day, that memory brings tears to my eyes. God has shown me who He is many times throughout my life, that He is indeed real and that He watches over us. That Father and daughter relationship is a direct reflection of both my physical and heavenly Father who have watched over, protected, and guided me. Even when I felt I had, in these moments, failed Him big time, His love never failed me. Our God is good. His love and mercy never change. He is the same God yesterday, today and forever.

Back to the Divination

This medicine you carry has been passed down from person to person to person: it's generational. I see Hopi ancestry in your lineage; they were seers and forecasters of the stars. They also knew deep knowledge about the transcendent and how mother earth moved through dimensions. There is a new hope to do it differently; there was something specifically passed down to you from a grandmother, a maternal great, great, great so far back great grandmother, from the Hopi side, she was an oracle, a healer.

You need to connect with her to find out more connect with her through dream. This is maternal; wait, father's side.

Pause

THE TRUTH I KNOW NOW

You don't need to connect with anyone but Jesus Christ. One of the key words here is "was": she *was* an oracle, *was* a healer. Past tense. Which tells me she is no longer. No thank you. These fly-by-night spiritual trends that people blindly follow are not only harmful, but they are no match for our Creator. He is the real deal. Depending on your own strength, power, or anything outside of God is Satan's way. From the very beginning, he wanted to be God. He believed he could stand on his own, be his own god—and we all know where that led him.

Today, people still fall for the same lie. We strive to be the best 'influencers,' relying on charisma and 'persuasiveness,' but this blinds us to the fact that many are working in the wrong kingdom. Don't be deceived. Even while in heaven Satan did this. He mastered persuasiveness, so much so that he persuaded one-third of the angels in heaven to join him in his rebellion against God—and they fell with him. One thing I can tell you that I know for sure: God is living, and

He reigns supreme.

Revelation 12:4,9
Its tail swept away a third of the stars in heaven and hurled them to the earth. So the great dragon was thrown out: the ancient serpent, who is called the devil and satan, the one who deceives the whole world. He was thrown to earth, and his angels with him.

Isaiah 14:12–15
Shining morning star, how you have fallen from the heavens! You destroyer of nations, you have been cut down to the ground. You said to yourself, "I will ascend to the heavens; I will set up my throne above the stars of God. I will sit on the mount of the god's assembly, in the remotest parts of the North. I will ascend above the highest clouds; I will make myself like the Most High." But you will be brought down to Sheol into the deepest regions of the Pit.

Back to the Divination

Hands. This has to do with your hands and deep prayer is what I'm getting. Deep prayer of the heart will be invoked in touch with the love and heart of God but it will also involve your hands as well.

This grandmother is going to teach you love: deep, deep love. Love on another level that you haven't experienced before. Because she is from the stars. She is a star being. It's going to shake your core and it's going to test you because her medicine is very powerful.

Pause

THE TRUTH I KNOW NOW

The gifts given by the Holy Spirit are sacred, bestowed for good works and for the building of God's Kingdom. Serve the Lord faithfully, and steward well what has been entrusted to you. God is love, and His teachings are sufficient. The blending of God's truth with occult practices was the way of the Chaldeans, the Amorites, and other nations—pagan traditions and forms of idolatry that led to separation from God. These ways are not new; they're just given new names. What was detestable to God then remains detestable in His sight. Your Creator's grace is sufficient.

1 Peter 4:10–11
Just as each one has received a gift, use it to serve others, as good stewards of the varied grace of God. If anyone speaks let it be as one who speaks God's words; if anyone serves, let it be from the strength God provides, so that God may be glorified through Jesus Christ in everything. To Him be the glory and the power forever and ever. Amen.

> **2 Kings 17:34 (NKJV)**
> To this day they continue practicing the former rituals; they do not fear the LORD or observe the statues and ordinances, or the law and commandment which the LORD had commanded the descendants of Jacob, whom He named Israel.
>
> **1 Kings 18:21**
> Then Elijah approached all the people and said, "How long will you waver between two opinions? If the LORD is God, follow Him. But if Baal, follow him."
>
> **Jeremiah 8:2–3**
> They will be exposed to the sun, the moon, and all the stars in the sky, which they have loved, served, followed, consulted, and worshipped. Their bones will not be collected and buried but will become like manure on the soil's surface. Death will be chosen over life by all the survivors of this evil family, those who remain wherever I have banished them. This is the declaration of the LORD of Armies.

Back to the Divination

You have to get clear, very clear, with yourself about what you want: you have to be honest with yourself about who you are and where you want to go. The direction going forward: very clear about why you are doing this, why you want to go down this route and this path. There is a certain level of certainty and clarity that needs to happen and that you need to sit through by writing and journaling and by clearing through the mirror and ask some questions. It's going to be challenging and it's going to rattle your bones, but it is going to give you that necessary shift and perspective of consciousness that you need to make the next step and to really know and understand whether this is the path you want to walk or not.

Once that is done, they are saying the guidance that is needed and required is waiting for you. But they are waiting because right now you are inhibiting the process you are wishy-washy: do I want it, do I not. You don't really know: the clarity is not fully present yet. The best thing to do at this point is to invoke the power that is within you and the power of God and the ancestors to give you the clarity that is needed and you have to pray.

Side Notes of an Experience

Not long after this divination, my husband and I stopped at a yard sale to check out some tools. I wandered over to a pile of old books. The first one I opened carried a message about the importance of life. The second book startled me more—inside were handwritten notes on the page that read:

Sometimes You look but You don't see.
Sometimes You hear but You don't listen.
Sometimes You care but you don't really.

I had a knowing that this message was spiritual. What I didn't realize then was that I stood at a spiritual crossroad. I was playing on the edge. I hadn't yet grasped what I was really doing, spiritually speaking. I wasn't anchored deeply enough in God's Word to understand the reality of what I was up against.

At the time, I wasn't clear on what any of the diviners were really talking about, I wasn't on the same page. I know, I know, trust me, I know—even as straightforward as it sounds and reads here, I was applying much of it to my physical life. Where I am with God now, rooted, I can see this very clearly for what it was. I met with that mirror on that morning call with my brother, the day my whole world came to a halt. That was the moment God spoke in a tone I pray He never has to use again. My eyes were opened that day. Still, I had a long run back to Him.

Back to the Divination

During the session, I was asked when I had last gone to the water—ocean or river. I replied by sharing an experience at the ocean that I had shortly after returning from the Elemental Immersion retreat:

The Blue Ball

When I returned from the retreat, I went to the ocean to pray and to cleanse a necklace I had received from one of the women there. Standing at the shore and looking out on the ocean, I noticed something drifting toward me from far out in the water. At first, I couldn't make it out, but it was moving directly toward me across the vast expanse.

As it got closer, I saw that it was a blue ball—similar to a medicine ball used for exercising. My first thought was that someone down the beach must have lost it. I glanced up and down the shoreline, expecting to see its owner, and prepared to grab it for them. But the beach was empty. It wasn't peak season, and that morning it was just me, my husband, and Savannah. No one else in sight. I didn't understand what was happening. But I knew with certainty that it was spiritual.

Back to the Divination

The reason this particular picture came up is they're saying the water is calling to you. The spirits of the water are calling to you. Yemoja is calling to you and you must answer her call: there is deep wisdom that the water has for you. And they know the path and the medicine in which you must walk. So, if you were to respond to their call, they will be able to get you to the altar or to the point of where you are going to reach the mountaintop.

The ball that was coming to you at the ocean was a symbol, it's like a sign from the water spirits: like they're gifting to you from themselves freely without any kind of attachment to it. And the fact that you were able to see the ball is in a way kind of miraculous.

They say to answer the call; you haven't answered the call yet. They gave you a message with the ball. What was the message? [I had no clue.] *You have to sit with it and trust yourself to know it. They're saying with you: you say you don't know, and you doubt, that is your comfortability, that is the little girl that still attaches and holds on to her father: that is a safe zone. You created this line of the safe zone of the little girl who is still attached to Father who doesn't want to be revealed to the unknown. When you are able to figure out the message of the ball that was gifted to you from yemoja, you will be able to freely step over into the other side and to the next path of your mission and medicine. I can't tell you the message; they won't give it to me. You will have to figure it out because it is a trust that you have to cultivate in yourself to understand it.*

I'm seeing two genies around you: do you work with genies? [I didn't know what that was outside the genie in Aladdin.] *There are two: one on each side of you. Are you going to Burkina?* [It's full, I said, but I'll still submit my application and if it's meant to happen, I'll be there.] *I get the sense of something about the Dargara and these particular genies: there is a connection. Since you were a child they have been there, they have been waiting patiently for the medicine you carry to activate, for you to be comfortable enough to step into your power and your knowing and for them to be able to assist in your work. I don't know what the work is. It will take time to figure it out, but the help is there I can see that the assistance from the other world is clearly and visibly there. And the protection is there. The next step is you stepping into the unknown and being okay with it. You have an interesting path, it will become clear to you: you are being guided by the voices from the other side, the elders, especially the water spirits.*

THE TRUTH I KNOW NOW

When I listen back to this, I cringe. It's as if I was wearing thick earmuffs—unable to truly hear what was being spoken to me, over me, and especially by *whom* I was being guided. There is nothing good, holy, or life-giving that can come from being led by voices from the dead, and especially water spirits—a very dangerous kingdom. They are not helpers—they are departed spirits and demons whose sole purpose is to guide you toward destruction with them.

> Galatians 5:7–10
> You were running well. Who prevented you from being persuaded regarding the truth? This persuasion does not come from the one who calls you. A little leaven leavens the whole batch of dough. I myself am persuaded in the LORD you will not accept any other view. But whoever it is that is confusing you will pay the penalty.

This is the danger of mixing God into these counterfeit spaces—it creates the illusion that it's safe, even blessed. But God is clear: *be as shrewd as serpents and innocent as doves.* And above all, test every spirit. Without being rooted in Christ and His Word, you are vulnerable to deception at increasingly high levels.

What does it mean to serve only one God? It means wholehearted allegiance. To love Him with all your heart, soul, mind, and strength. To worship Him alone, not seeking guidance or provision from other sources. To give Him our obedience and loyalty in every area of our lives.

> **Deuteronomy 6:13–14**
> Fear the LORD your God, worship him, and take your oaths in his name. Do not follow other gods, the gods of the peoples around you.
>
> **Matthew 22:37**
> He said to him, "Love the LORD your God with all your heart, with all your soul, and with all your mind. This is the greatest and most important command."
>
> **Exodus 20:3–5**
> Do not have other gods besides me. Do not make an idol for yourself, whether in the shape of anything in the heavens above or on the earth below or in the waters under the earth. Do not bow in worship to them, and do not serve them; for I, the LORD your God, am a jealous God.
>
> **Hosea 4:6**
> My people are destroyed for lack of knowledge.

The Holy Spirit has shown me that, yes, I am a leader of a people in God's Kingdom. The spiritual gifts I carry belong to Him, for they were given by Him for the good of His people and to stand firm in the fight of faith. Yes, I am a warrior: not by my own strength, but by the power of God who equips me. I have been uniquely shaped and prepared by the Lord for His purpose. These gifts were protected and perhaps hidden for a time such as this, to serve His people: to advance His Kingdom alongside the body of Christ, and to fulfill His will for my life. And through Jesus Christ, I am a repairer of broken walls and a restorer of unity among His people.

The enemy knows the gifts you carry. He studies the body of Christ—every trauma, every unhealed wound, any angle that he can exploit to attack. His goal is always the same: to throw you off the path that God has set before you, to delay your blessings, to rob you of the goodness prepared for you. Don't let him. Don't hand over what God has promised you just because the enemy lost his place in heaven.

Keep in step with the Holy Spirit, and when the accuser comes against you, put him back in his place under the authority of Christ—for the battle has already been won by the blood of the Lamb.

Revelation 12:11
They conquered him by the blood of the Lamb and by the word of their testimony; for they did not love their lives to the point of death.

Isaiah 58:10–12
If you offer yourself to the hungry and satisfy the afflicted one then your light will shine in the darkness, and your night will become like noonday. The Lord will always lead you,

satisfy you in a parched land, and strengthen your bones. You will be like a watered garden. And like a spring whose water never runs dry. Some of you will rebuild the ancient ruins; you will restore the foundations laid long ago; you will be called the repairer of broken walls, the restorer of streets where people live.

Romans 8:28
We know that all things work together for the good of those who love God, who are called according to his purpose.

Even here—even in this—God has turned it for the good.

Reiki and Crystal Phase

I was searching for a place to purchase authentic crystals when I met a woman by what seemed like fate. The town her shop was located in happened to share the same name as a town near my home. My husband actually found this shop for me, and we both thought it was local. Turns out it was upstate New York. Still, I looked it up, and it seemed authentic enough, so I made the trip. When I arrived, I walked in and was greeted by the owner—except she called me by someone else's name. She must have read my expression of confusion and quickly explained, "Oh, I'm sorry, I thought you were the woman scheduled for an appointment. Excuse me a second while I call her." A moment later she returned and said the woman had canceled. I couldn't help but think it was interesting timing. I had been planning to get a reading if the atmosphere felt right, and now, with the scheduled client absent—that should have been the woman walking through the door at this time, felt almost as if the opening had been meant for me. It seemed so, but I held my reserve.

We began to talk, and the conversation flowed easily, and felt genuine—as if I had known her for years. She carried herself with such warmth, and I could sense she was a good soul. We discovered many similarities in our lives and experiences, and she even remarked that I resembled her mother, who had recently passed. But the moment that sealed the connection was when I mentioned how my Dad sends a Bible passage to the family group chat every morning by 7 a.m. She lit up and said, "What?! My Dad does too!" We both froze, looked at each other and then at the same time asked: "What's your Dad's name?" before either of us said a word we burst into laughter. We didn't share the same father, but the bond of the moment was undeniable.

I decided to get a reading. Afterward, she handed me a Scripture passage to read and hyssop to bathe in. I remember thinking, *Why is she giving me Scripture?* It was strange, as I hadn't seen anyone give Scripture in these spaces. It left me a little unsettled: *Why are you mixing God with this?* Still, I took it—and I even booked a Reiki class she recommended that was happening that weekend.

REIKI CLASS: DAY 1

When the weekend came, I showed up bright and early for the two-day Reiki training. The first day seemed harmless enough. We went over the history of Reiki, and then we were given some homework: to memorize the Reiki healing symbols and a set of affirmations:

> Just for today, do not worry.
> Just for today, do not anger.
> Just for today, honor your parents, teachers, and elders.
> Just for today, earn a living honestly.
> Just for today, show gratitude for everything.

One the surface, it all sounded good—a nice little moral compass. I thought to myself: *This isn't dark; maybe Reiki healing is okay after all?* But the very next part unsettled me deep in my spirit. Before practicing Reiki, we were instructed to recite this affirmation: "Dear master Usui and all other available Reiki masters: Please guide and assist me in becoming a pure channel for your loving Reiki energy. And provide me with whatever protection I may need. Thank you and Amen."

This didn't sit well with me. My spirit stirred with unease. Instead of saying this I made up my own version: "Dear Usui, practitioner of Reiki healing. Highest most aligned divine, I call on you to guide and assist me in becoming a pure channel for your loving Reiki energy. Dear God Almighty Creator of Heaven and Earth watch over and protect me in this space. Amen."

THE TRUTH I KNOW NOW

The very thing I was questioning—why are they mixing God with this?—I was guilty of myself. That's exactly what I was doing. Mixing God into practices that had nothing to do with Him. Adding His name into the ritual didn't make it holy. It didn't sanctify it. My so-called "fixed" version was still not the way of God—it was just *my version* of how I wanted Him to fit into my life at that time.

Deuteronomy 12:30–31
Be careful not to be ensnared by their ways after they have been destroyed before you. Do not inquire about their gods, asking, 'How did these nations worship their gods?' I'll do the same. You must not

> do the same to the Lord your God, because they practice every detestable act, which the Lord hates, for their gods.
>
> Isaiah 42:8–9
> "I am the Lord, that is my name, and I will not give my glory to another or my praise to idols. The past events have indeed happened. Now I declare new events; I announce them to you before they occur."

REIKI CLASS: DAY 2

The day began after a good night's rest. After prayer and meditation, I noticed a blue jay land on a branch outside my window. During this time, I still believed that animals carried messages of spiritual guidance. That blue jay, to me, meant: Be fearless. According to one of the spiritual animal guidebooks I leaned on during this time, the blue jay could also symbolize lessons about not allowing yourself to be placed in a position where power is misused against you.

The drive upstate was peaceful. I remember looking out the window and seeing an eagle soaring high above the mountains, and later while taking my exit, there was a white horse standing perfectly still in a wide-open field of lush green grass. It was the only horse in sight, and it stood so still I had to slow down, blink, and look again to be sure it was real—it looked majestic.

When I arrived, the vibe was chill—light and welcoming. We even met the shop owner's child, who brought such sweet, pure energy into the space. Day two was all about the energy practice. This part was always difficult for me. I was very sensitive to people spiritually, and engaging in exercises where you exchanged or worked with each other's energy often left me feeling heavy and drained. It took a lot just for me to stay in that type of environment. Deep down, I still hadn't made up my mind about this part of the practice, regarding whether or not I would be participating.

The instructor announced that we would be paired by twos. It was a small group, so the arrangement made sense. But as soon as she said it, I already knew who I hoped to be paired with—and more importantly, who I absolutely did not want to be paired with. I trusted the instructor would sense what I was picking up on. And of course, who did I get paired with? The very person I told myself I would not work with. I scanned my thoughts: *Did I really want to be that person and hurt her feelings? Will I look like the difficult one? Am I overreacting, just thinking too much?* I wrestled with it. *Maybe I should just push through—I'm protected, it'll be fine.* I didn't want to disrupt the class. But then the final thought cut through everything: *No. Absolutely not—it's not happening.*

At first, I kept quiet. Our turn was supposed to be first. But when I glanced over at her, I noticed something was off—her body was restless, her eyes glossy, as if she was battling something unseen. The instructor noticed too and asked if she was okay. She gave the next pair the chance to go first to give her time to get herself together. Many things were going through my mind at this point. Inside, I was torn. *Is she okay? Maybe I'm supposed to help her. Maybe that's why we were paired. I know I'm protected—I'll be fine.* But again, the same firm conviction: *No. Not happening.*

When it was almost our turn, she grew visibly emotional. Suddenly, she jumped up, ran to the backroom, and we all heard loud sobs and panicked hyperventilation. The whole room shifted—but not me. I just watched, recognizing what my spirit had already told me. The instructor quickly stepped in to comfort her, then returned to the group and asked everyone if they could grab their things, walk down the block to get some air, regroup, and meet her at a nearby ice cream shop. She asked me to stay behind.

She was skilled at clearing the space and resetting the tone. During our walk to meet up with the others, she shared that she felt the outburst was due to her feeling intimidated by my power. At the time, I interpreted it through the lens of ancestors and spiritual strength, believing it was my light and the light of my ancestors shining powerfully. Spiritually, what she carried could not stand in my presence in this space. I shared with her what I felt before the pairing, hoping she would have picked it up. I also shared the blue jay sighting that morning and the message I believed it to carry then: not allowing yourself to be placed in position where power is misused against you.

THE TRUTH I KNOW NOW

I understand now what was really happening. It was never my power or light. What she carried could not stand in the presence of the Holy Spirit that dwells within God's people. The conviction, the power, the light—that was Him, and had nothing to do with me. When someone's spirit is unclean, the Holy Spirit can bring about a sense of conviction regarding their wrongdoing. The conviction serves as a gentle nudge from the Holy Spirit to prompt them to acknowledge their sin, seek forgiveness, and turn away from their wrongful ways.

> **John 16:7–11**
> "Nevertheless, I am telling you the truth. It is for your benefit that I go away, because if I don't go away the Counselor will not come to you. If I go, I will send him to you. When he comes, he will convict the world about sin, righteousness, and judgment: About sin, because they do not believe in me; about righteousness, because I am going to the Father and you will no longer see me; and about judgment, because the ruler of this world has been judged."

You Are a Reflection of Jesus Christ and God's Kingdom

I ended up working with two classmates, a male and a female, and we connected easily. Together, we practiced energy therapy. The person receiving the healing energy would lie flat on their back, while the practitioner scanned from head to toe, hands hovering just above the body. When the session ended, the practitioner would share what they had "received," whether it was a vision, feeling, a thought or sometimes nothing at all. This was not far-fetched for me at the time. I could naturally sense and see in the spirit. It was fascinating to watch how precise some of these were. One girl, before sharing with the wider group, asked her partner privately if she was pregnant—because that's what she had picked up. The woman confirmed that she had only been a few weeks along.

This is what was shared with me after my scan:

Pastures, blue/teal big ocean water.
Huge bird wings spread wide at my crown.
The color green.
"Get comfortable" being heard.
White, really bright light.

I couldn't help but connect it with the eagle I had seen soaring across the sky on my drive that morning. Later when I got home, I looked up the spiritual meaning of "pastures," curious why that would come up for me.

Now remember, during this time in my life I wasn't rooted in God's Word. The opening of Psalm 23 is one of the most well-known passages in Scripture—yet back then, "pastures" didn't ring any bell for me. That's how dry my well was. I wasn't anchored in the Word then, so instead of opening my Bible, I turned to a search engine. And this is what came back:

Psalm 23:1–4 (KJV)
The L͟o͟r͟d͟ is my Shepherd; I shall not want. He maketh me to lie down in green pastures: he leadeth me beside still waters. He restoreth my soul: he leadeth me in the paths of righteousness for his name's sake. Yes, though I walk through the valley of the shadow of death, I will fear no evil: for thou art with me; thy rod and thy staff they comfort me.

And that morning drive came rushing back to my mind—the details I had overlooked now glowed with significance. The drive was peaceful, I saw an eagle soaring high above the mountains. The white horse—majestic, unmoving, standing alone in acres of lush, green pastures. And the bright light that the owner shared with me in private with regard to the outburst. God is so good. Even in those places, God never left me.

THE TRUTH I KNOW NOW

Revelation 19:11–16
Then I saw heaven opened, and there was a white horse. Its rider is called Faithful and True, and with justice he judges and makes war. His eyes were like fiery flame, and many crowns were on his head. He had a name written that no one knows except himself. He wore a robe dipped in blood, and his name is called the Word of God. The armies that were in heaven followed him on white horses, wearing pure white linen. A sharp sword came from his mouth, so

> that he might strike the nations with it. He will rule them with an iron rod. He will also trample the winepress of the fierce anger of God, the Almighty. And he has a name written on his robe and on his thigh: King of Kings and LORD of Lords.
>
> ### Isaiah 40:28,30-31
> Do you know? Have you not heard? The LORD is the everlasting God, the Creator of the whole earth. He never becomes faint or weary; there is no limit to his understanding. Youths may become faint and weary, and young men stumble and fall, but those who trust in the LORD will renew their strength; they will soar on wings like eagles, they will run and not become weary, they will walk and not faint.

I still tear up when I think about how intentional, how detailed, and how precise God has been with my life. Writing this book and sharing my testimony is not an easy thing. You open yourself to the world, exposing the most vulnerable parts of your story—the shame, the embarrassment of falling for these pagan ways. You put yourself in the seat to be judged. And as a deeply private person, I prayed many nights for God to help me press through. Because in the end, I know His glory is bigger than my comfort. If this journey helps even one person find their way back to Him, back home, then it is worth it all. The truth and the love of God are immeasurable and truly unmatched.

If you remember, the first day I met the owner of the shop, she gave me herbs, a candle, and a Scripture passage following my reading. My "remedy" was to bathe in the hyssop and read the passage aloud. But I didn't. Not that night. Not for a few days. Something in me held off—I couldn't explain why. I wasn't feeling led to follow through. My senses told me: wait.

White as Snow: Psalm 51

A week later, the time came when I decided to follow through with the spiritual bath that had been "prescribed." It was simple: hyssop, dead sea salt, and Psalm 51 read from the heart. When I got to a particular line, I hesitated. The words "white as snow" caught in my throat. And at the end, "in Jesus' name I pray"—I stumbled there too. But I said it. I spoke it out. The experience was emotional, and when I finished, I went downstairs. From the kitchen window, I froze. The view outside looked different, as if the world itself had shifted. I opened the door, stepped out, and the deck was covered in snow—yes, snow. It was the first snowfall of the season, and we were one day away from March—very late for our region. I wanted to drop to my knees, but it was too cold. Still, right there, I gave God the glory in Jesus' name. He is so faithful. His love is truly unmatched.

Side Note

This is another embarrassing part of my journey, but it needs to be shared. The reason I hesitated at those words—"white as snow" and "in Jesus' name I pray"—was rooted in a wound. Let's be honest: racism is real. Systemic racism runs deep in our nation's fabric, and it exists across every race. But the real prison is the mind—the narratives we accept that keep us divided and bound.

As a biracial woman, I've lived in the tension of both sides. I've seen the ugliness of both. And the truth is this: at the core, we share the same insecurities, the same struggles, the same longing for love. Yes, anything divided will fall—and that has always been the enemy's plan. Sadly, many people feed into the lies that keep us divided.

Growing up, I often felt caught in the middle, never fully belonging anywhere. I still remember when I didn't even have a box to check for my race when filling out official forms. That feeling of "no place to call home" runs deep, I'm sure, for all biracial people. And at one point, it twisted into my faith. I questioned why Jesus was always depicted as white, why African history was constantly erased, diminished, or dismissed. Out of that wound, I entertained the thought that Jesus was unnecessary—a third party I didn't need to reach God. I opted at that time to just go straight to the source: why did I need a messenger? But that was ignorance and my immaturity in the Word.

I love Jesus Christ now. He has shown me more than I could ever deserve. He is our Lord and Savior, sitting at the right hand of the Father, interceding for us day and night. He loved me even when I didn't love or acknowledge Him. God warns us about creating images and idols for a reason: *make nothing in the heavens above or on earth below.* Yet it amazes me how many church establishments do this—using images of Jesus, setting up statues of all kinds, even of mother Mary, and in some cases even kneeling before them as a representation and worship. That is the very definition of an idol. God help us. I often wonder, are they reading a different version of the Bible … or are they reading it at all?

Exodus 20:2–5
I am the LORD your God, who brought you out of the land of Egypt, out of the place of slavery. Do not have other gods besides me. Do not make an idol for yourself, whether in the shape of anything in the heavens above or on the earth below or in the waters under the earth. Do no bow in worship to them, and do not serve them for I, the LORD your God am a jealous God.

John 14:6
Jesus told him, "I am the way, the truth, and the life. No one comes to the Father except through me."

Acts 17:26–27
From one man he has made every nationality to live over the whole earth and has determined their appointed times and the boundaries of where they live. He did this so that they might seek God, and perhaps they might reach out and find Him, though He is not far from each one of us.

I've shared these parts and transitions in my life during my time of seeking God to show that it took time, there was a purification process—a peeling away of all that was not of Him. I was mixing God with other occult practices, thinking it was okay. It was not. I still had a long way to go, but the Holy Spirit was leading me out of the confusion, lifting the veil so I could see the truth.

Jeremiah 29:13–14
"You will seek me and find me when you search for me with all your heart. I will be found by you."

Proverbs 3:5–6 (NKJV)
Trust in the LORD with all your heart, and lean not on your own understanding; in all your ways acknowledge Him, and He shall direct your paths.

Isaiah 55:8
"For my thoughts are not your thoughts, and your ways are not my ways."

My Cry Out to God

During my time of seeking, I still felt something was off. I had no peace. On the outside I was put together, like everything was beautiful—but inside, my spirit was crying out. Something just wasn't right, and deep down, I knew it. My spirit kept nudging me. That morning, before my quiet time, I went to the bedroom window to raise the shade. As I did, a blue jay flew past and perched on the tree, the sunlight was glistening through the branches into my eyes. In that moment, I heard in my spirit: *Keep your head to the sky.* I sat down to just be still, but instead of the calm I was searching for, I cried out. With tears streaming, I prayed: "God, creator of heaven and earth, help me." That was all I could say—*help*. I didn't even know with what or why, but I trusted that He knew. He knows our heart and intentions. I asked Him to help me through this. Then I sat there—crying, still, listening. As I moved through the day preparing to take Savannah out for our morning run—I noticed that we had gotten off to a late start and that this day was hot. I checked my phone before we got started and the day's Scripture was the first message there waiting to be opened. This morning's message was longer than usual. I would usually just save it for later, but my eyes locked on the word shining brighter than anything else in the text (the word "help") … and this is what it said:

Dad's Morning Scripture

Morning family, you know what time it is. Today's bible

verse comes from the book of **2 Corinthians 6:2; vs2**- For He saith, I have heard thee in a time accepted, and in the Day of Salvation have I succored thee: **(help)** behold now is the accepted time; behold now is the day of Salvation: Amen.

Our Salvation rests upon this. Paul quoted Isaiah in his epistle to the Corinthians when he wrote: "we also urge you not to receive the Grace of God in vain-for He says, 'at the acceptable time I listened to you, and on the day of Salvation I helped you.'" God helped His people when He sent Jesus to save His people from their sin-to die on the cross pay the price for their sin and rise again on the third day. ALL THEY HAVE TO DO IS TO BELIEVE. Amen. until tomorrow, have a bless day, and always keep the faith, and our LORD God will always keep you. Amen.

What I know for sure is I serve a living God. He is watching over you ever so closely.

IDENTITY

By this point, my mother and father had been caring for my grandmother—our Mum-Mum—for eight years. After a minor stroke, she was no longer as sharp as she once had been. Still, she was fiercely independent and deeply conscious of not wanting to become a burden to anyone. To honor her wishes my Dad monitored her closely while she remained in her home, but after a few close calls, my parents made the decision to bring her to live with them. Even then, for many years, she managed most things on her own. She only needed supervision. My Mom was still working during this time, which meant that my parents had to divide the load—my Dad took the mornings with Mum-Mum, and my Mom took the evenings. Together, they carried it. I watched them. Day in and day out, I saw the sacrifices they made. I helped where I could, but this was their everyday—the daily weight was theirs to bear. Over the years, it took its toll—especially on my Mom. Not only physically and mentally, but I'm sure spiritually as well.

In late 2023 Mum-Mum's health started to decline, and it happened quickly. She went from moving on her own, to needing some help, to requiring round-the-clock care. My Mom had always vowed never to place her in a nursing facility, and when the time came, she kept that vow. She did whatever it took to care for her at home. She brought in hospice and bore the responsibility on their shoulders. I had always known my Mom to be a strong woman, but this was a different strength. I didn't know this side of her, but I deeply respected it. I remember telling her at times that I feared if she kept going at that pace, Mum-Mum might outlive her. I could see the exhaustion etched in her face, yet she refused to give in. I admired her for that—for the way she carried a mountain of responsibility: without having all the answers, she pressed on anyway.

I always told my Mom that once she retired, I would take her traveling to see the world. At that time, she had never been anywhere, and I wanted her to experience life beyond caregiving. Mum-Mum was with her well into retirement, and travel was out of the question. My Dad was a rock in supporting her. He did all the manly things he could do to help around the clock. Day and night, steady and dependable. During Mum-Mum's time on hospice, she required constant care. Now understand—my Mum-Mum was a tough cookie: independent, strong, and a woman of integrity. Needing full dependence on someone else I'm sure wasn't easy for her. Yet the care my Mom gave was nothing short of impeccable. I remember one weekend taking a trip home to help, but this morning I just sat watching my Mom as she cared for her mother. I couldn't help but smile. She was remarkable—better than any nurse I've ever seen. She was like a special nurse handpicked just for her. There was never a day when Mum-Mum didn't smell fresh and clean. My Mom made sure of it. I was proud of my parents. Watching them, helping where I could, through this time I stood taller. I was proud to be their child. What I witnessed in that season was love in action. Selfless humility. True duty.

Side Note

I share this story to show how God has a funny way of turning things around. My Mom told me she always wanted to be a nurse when she grew up. When my mother was young, she came home from school one day full of excitement. She told her Mom that she wanted to be a nurse. But instead of encouragement, she was told she couldn't do it—and that she was needed at home to help around the house and watch over her brother and sister.

My Mom told me this story when I was a child. It was part

of her "you can do anything" pep talk. Even then, I remember thinking how crushing that would feel—to have your dream or goals dismissed by someone you loved, someone you trusted. What's even more heartbreaking is that she believed her. She never pursued nursing. This was the work of the enemy, a lie from the darkest pit to cripple her imagination while it was at its peak. But God has the last say. How interesting that He positioned this very same woman—my mother—to be the "nurse" she at one point in her life had dreamed to be. And it was no coincidence who her very first patient would be: her mother.

Now it was my mother's choice to believe the lie back then—God gives us free will. But He is still the author and the finisher. His Word does not return void. In His perfect timing, He exposed that lie and shone His light on the truth, so that both could see it. Never let the enemy steal what God has spoken and ordained for your life.

Maternal Family History

During this time, lots of family came to visit. We were all home more, surrounding Mum-Mum with love. One day my great-uncle and great-aunt came over to see their sister—she's the eldest of the three. When I told Mum-Mum that her brother was there to see her, her whole face lit up. Her smile was so wide that it filled the room with joy—she loved her brother. It always reminds me of how I feel about my brothers.

When they arrived, my great-aunt brought me a photo of my great grandmother, their mother, and a stack of very old family photos. I was filled with so much joy, holding those pieces of history in my hands. It was the kind of family time everyone needs; the kind we too often reserve for moments like this. I suppose we don't truly grasp the value of time until it slips away.

My great-uncle began sharing stories of our family history. His memory was sharp as a tack, and he even spoke some German. That was one thing Mum-Mum and I shared, speaking to each other in German—keeping her mind sharp and stirring memories of her childhood. He told me how our great-grandparents traveled from Germany to the U.S., how they met, and how their mother was the best baker. With a tender smile, he said, "She made the best German chocolate cake." I could see the love in his eyes as he shared the family stories. His next story sent chills down my spine.

He began by sharing something I'll never forget: that the family's real last name was originally a Jewish name—something like Kotowski. I leaned in, listening closely, scribbling notes as he pronounced it the best he could. I spelled it the way it sounded to me. He went on to explain that our great-grandfather and his family changed the name to a more German-sounding one so they could fit in and go under the radar during Hitler's time. Back then, family records in Germany were kept in churches. The church my family attended eventually burned down, destroying those records. It was in that gap that their names—their identities—were altered for survival.

I sat frozen, my mouth hanging open. My mind immediately flashed back to a dream I'd had two years earlier. When I got home, I searched through my dream journals and found it written there. Reading my own handwriting brought me to tears. I didn't know what to do with it all—the timing, the connection—it was overwhelming.

DREAM: IDENTITY

I had this dream in July 2021, two years before this family revelation was shared with me. I was once told that one of my gifts was *duality*. Not knowing what that meant, before bed that night I asked "my ancestors" to show me what that meant, and how I can use it to help people.

That night I dreamt I was in harm's way; I was trying to escape and was being chased. I came to an abandoned car. I climbed in to hide, and a war tank pulled up in front of the car and aimed its cannon at it, ready to blow it up. I quickly jumped out and turned to find my childhood close friends reaching out for help. I went back and grabbed her, but I couldn't save the other, she was in shock and limp, so I had to carry her—it felt like I carried her for miles! I was exhausted (even in waking I was breathing heavy and sweating). I came to a familiar house that I knew, spiritually I guess, I knew I'd been there before and that I would be safe. I went to the basement to hide my friend and walk around to make sure no one else was there. In one of the bedrooms, I found a little Caucasian boy. I felt I knew him; he definitely knew me—he smiled and started talking. I tried to hush him because he was talking loud with excitement and as I turned, I was faced with a Caucasian woman, his mother, and she said "Oh hi Ivonne?" And I quickly replied "Yes Ivonne Penny"—I knew this was a fake name and I said it as if I said it before and went by it.

My duality in that moment saved our lives. She believed me to be an identity or race that I was not.

THE TRUTH I KNOW NOW

When we don't live in the fullness of who we are in Christ, we live in survival mode—constantly running, hiding, and adapting to environments never meant to define us. Without knowing our true identity, we create false ones just to make it through the day.

But in Christ, we are more than conquerors. We are not meant to live small or uncertain of who we are, but to walk boldly in the authority given to us as sons and daughters of the Most High God. The enemy can only steal what we do not claim. No more running—stand firm on the Word of God, for in Him we are safe, known, and whole.

Ephesians 2:10 (NKJV)
For we are His workmanship, created in Christ Jesus for good works, which God prepared beforehand that we should walk in them.

Luke 10:19 (NKJV)
"Behold, I have given you authority to tread on serpents and scorpions, and over all the power of the enemy, and nothing shall by any means hurt you."

MUM-MUM'S PASSING

Three weeks later, our Mum-Mum passed away. I was planning to come home that weekend so we could all celebrate my Mom's birthday. I knew in my heart this might be her last birthday with her Mom—and possibly my last visit with my Mum-Mum. I had everything packed and planned: our party cone hats, the camera ready for good pictures, thinking of the memories we would make and capture. My husband, Savannah, and I were packed and ready to drive down the next day. When I went to bed that night I had a dream.

Dream: The Gathering

I dreamt of a gathering. There were lots of people and family. I saw my brother Marlin and his wife. It was raining a light rain, and I was walking with three other people. I said I needed to grab another umbrella so we could all be covered. The man next to me said it's okay, we'll be okay. In the dream I knew the people I was walking with but in waking I could not recall.

Messages

I woke up at 6 a.m. to messages from my Mom. When I called, she said that Mum-Mum's breathing had changed. I didn't like the tone of her voice, so I told her, "I'll pack the car and leave now." I rushed downstairs to pack; the sun wasn't up yet and the house was still dark. As I stepped into the kitchen, I suddenly felt a pause in my spirit: *Be still.*

I walked out on the deck to calm myself and watch the sunrise. And as I stepped on the deck before the sunrise, a quiet drizzle was falling. If felt like time stood still—like my dream had slipped into the physical. It was the light rain that brought me back to recalling the dream. I sat in a chair, closed my eyes, and prayed. The part of the prayer I remember was this: "Whatever is happening, I am okay. I am at peace."

When I finished, I gathered my bags, went upstairs to freshen up and woke my husband. "We're leaving early," I said. There was no time to wait for him—I felt an urgency to go.

Savannah jumped in the car, and we headed home.

By the time my husband woke up and called me, I was almost home. I told him about the dream, the quiet rain, and the urgency I felt to leave to get home early to see her. I told him that even though I had prepared myself, every time I thought of her, all I wanted was to see her smile and hear her soft whispers—words she tried so hard to form as her body grew weaker.

I made it home and when I pulled into the driveway, I saw many cars. It was too early for this many cars, I thought. I saw my Dad and my oldest brother, Duane, standing outside in the driveway. My first sense was: *Something isn't right.* I waved and drove around to the other side of the driveway to park. By then, my Dad was gone, and my brother was still there sitting in his car. This was extra strange, as my Dad always greets me when I pull up. As soon as I stepped out, the feeling deepened—something was off. My brother got out and started walking toward me; I asked what was going on, why were there so many cars. He didn't answer me, he just wrapped his arms around me and hugged me tight. I asked, "What's wrong?" and he wouldn't say anything, he only held me closer. And in that silence—I felt it through him—she was gone; I didn't make it in time.

Time has a way of showing us how quickly plans can shift into a new reality. We wept and we cried together. My mind spun, trying to grasp that I would never again see her eyes meet mine or her beautiful smile light up her face. That was it—she was gone. In the house my Mom, holding back tears, told me she had passed in the morning.

The next morning, I woke early. I sat in the sunroom where Mum-Mum used to be. The room was still. I closed my eyes to feel and while resting my eyes in the stillness and missing my mumsie a mourning bird appeared on the skylight window. It looked down at me and all around the room and then proceeded to the window closest to me. Two more appeared—as if together, like family. I laughed and felt a sense of peace.

I took Savannah out and she pulled me insistently to walk around the house. Normally, I would've taken her back in, but that morning, I followed. We came around to the front of the house, where the sun was gently lighting the grass. The stillness was almost holy. When I looked up, the tree in the yard was full of the mourning birds that had visited me in the sunroom. In that moment I felt a presence. It looked like guardians and protectors surrounding our home. It was a beautiful sight.

When walking back into the house, I paused and glanced down at the garden stone that had always been there. I wasn't sure why it caught my attention so strongly that morning, but it read: *Faith*. That garden stone had been there for years, yet something called my attention to see it differently this morning.

I thought about a woman I connected with named Faith a few weeks ago—and how Faith seemed to be God's theme for me that season.

Later that day I received a text message. I received a text from Faith:

Faith: Hi Britt, I just wanted you to know I'm thinking of you. I hope you are feeling strong and clear for the road ahead. Lots of love sister.

Me: Hi Faith, telepathy was for sure at work this morning. I thought of you when passing my Mom's garden steppingstone early this morning and took a pause in gratitude. My grandmother passed early Saturday morning, so my focus has been with her. It's been a draining few days. Thank you, Faith. I felt your love and you were right on time.

Faith: Oh wow, that's so much to hold … you are being surrounded by angels right now, and you are never alone.

I had met Faith a few weeks earlier, when reaching out to her for a Reiki session. But it was unlike any session I'd ever experienced—she carried an almost angelic presence. I remember her praying to the third heaven during our session. I had a knowing of this place deep within my spirit. At the time, we were going through similar life circumstances, and I knew our meeting was no coincidence.

THE TRUTH I KNOW NOW

2 Corinthians 12:2

I know a man in Christ who was caught up to the third heaven fourteen years ago. Whether he was in the body or out of the body, I don't know; God knows.

It was like she could see right through me—past the walls, straight to the heartbreak I thought I had buried long ago. She told me of the protection that surrounded me, how powerful it was. And how much the angels believed in me. Then she spoke about my throat: how there had been an attempt to silence me. During our call, I went into a vision. Before me appeared a church—an old schoolhouse church. I could see it vividly. I have seen this church in a vision before. There are other details I have chosen not to disclose. This is the dream I had the night after this session:

DREAM: WALKING ON SNAKES

I dreamt I was walking through some type of waterway or swamp type of place. There was a deep ocean runoff to my left. I was very conscious to stay on the right side, not to fall off into the deepest part of the water. I was in an ancient time and the number 33 was present. When I looked down, I saw three snakes, their bodies were massive: not like the size of snakes in this world. I could only see the thickness of the bodies underneath my feet as I walked through a water passage. The water passage I was walking spanned miles in length. There were high mountains, water, and lots of green hanging moss.

THE TRUTH AND WHAT I KNOW NOW

God was with me in the valley and through the waters. He protected me in the wilderness, and the rivers did not overwhelm me. My God.

Deuteronomy 8:15
He led you through the great and terrible wilderness with its poisonous snakes and scorpions, a thirsty land where there was no water.

Isaiah 43:1–2
"Do not fear, for I have redeemed you; I have called you by your name; you are mine. When you pass through the waters, I will be with you, and the rivers will not overwhelm you."

Luke 10:19 (NKJV)
"Behold, I have given you the authority to trample on snakes and scorpions and over all the power of the enemy; and nothing shall by any means hurt you."

Psalm 23:4 (NKJV)
Yea, though I walk through the valley of the shadow of death, I will fear no evil; for You are with me; Your rod and Your staff, they comfort me.

THE FALL FROM PSEUDO-GRACE

I had reached so many heights in my life, shattered personal ceilings I never thought possible. I was on top of the world, creating the life I envisioned. However:

> "At your highest moment, be careful, that's when the devil comes for you."
> —Denzel Washington

I call it a fall from pseudo-grace because it was a life 'I' created. I had left out the most important ingredient: God. Through all the milestones and wins, I was forgetting the most valuable player. Can you imagine, in our limited understanding, doing so much for someone and never receiving a thank you—never even being acknowledged? It's like a ship sailing smoothly across the sea, never realizing or acknowledging the lighthouse that has guided it safely through every storm. Sadly, many only turn their attention to God when life goes wrong. But the truth is: God sustains us through it all. Even when we make our own decisions apart from His way or will for our lives. Let's not forget the reason you are still breathing this very moment is because God Almighty has allowed it.

PART TWO

When the Veil Was Lifted

Sprinting Back to God

By this time, it had been almost eight months since the call with my brother—and me sitting in God's warning. That call woke me up from a deep spiritual slumber. Up until this point, I still hadn't fully known what was right or wrong, or how far I had traveled away from Him.

On this night, I couldn't sleep. I was up scrolling and though I had an early day ahead it didn't help me sleep. Little did I know, this night into morning was about to change my life. What unfolded in the morning rocked my reality again. The difference between this encounter and the call with my brother was that it exposed everything that I thought was good and true. The occult practices and spiritualty that I had been following were revealed in a woman's testimony, and I was left speechless.

Around 2 a.m., a video appeared in my YouTube feed. I didn't know why, but I felt nudged to watch it. I wasn't a follower of the channel, and I didn't know of the woman who was sharing her story. What I saw was so moving—so revealing—that it exposed the lies that up until that point I believed were harmless and were part of "my walk with God." In reality it showed just how far, in every detail, I had drifted from God. I couldn't integrate it all at that very moment. But I knew the video hadn't shown up by chance. When the video ended, I really couldn't go to sleep. I wasn't sure what to do next—whether to reach out to her, or if my message would even get through. I imagined she must be flooded with messages from others who had seen the video. After sitting for a bit, I decided to message her and leave it at that. I didn't know what exactly to say, but I knew I needed to speak to her. I sent the message, only realizing afterward that it was now 3 a.m.; I thought, *She's going to think I'm insane.* To my surprise, when I went back to the chat she had replied immediately. I checked her time zone—UK time—and realized it was about 8 a.m. for her. Relief washed over me. I tried to get some sleep, finally dozing off at 4 a.m. I slept for about three hours. That morning, I had a cleaner coming to steam and clean the sofas, but my mind picked up right where it had left off before dozing off a few hours ago. I didn't want to do anything but talk to the woman.

I woke up to the sun shining directly on my face. It felt still and intentional, like a promise from God: *I am with you.* As I lay there, still thinking about the video and the deception, I couldn't ignore the sun. It was so bright; shining down on me, it grew brighter and bigger, and I then had a knowing in my spirit: *I have never left you.* In that moment, it was like energy surged through me and I felt like singing: I jumped up and sang: "My God is an awesome God, He reigns!" I couldn't tell you why, but the words poured out of me as I ran upstairs singing throughout the house.

A couple days later, during Savannah's morning routine, I opened the front door and found a dead bird lying on the entryway. I froze. Part of me didn't want to read into it, but deep down I knew—it was a spiritual response—a warning. Still, I brushed it off, grabbed gloves and asked my husband to discard it. That night I went into a dream of what that response meant.

DREAM: THE SPIRITUAL WAR FOR MY SOUL

I had a dream of the ocean. This ocean was massive: as far as the eye could see. The tidal flow was steady going in and out, rising and receding like a pulse. My husband was there, and he had his phone to his ear. I would warn him when there was a strong incoming tide so he had time to take cover and run to the land. This happened about one or two times: the waves and tide at that time were bearable. Then the water started to recede far back, and a huge portion of the ocean floor was exposed. In the distance I could see an army, they were standing far back where the receding stopped in the water. There were many army men dressed in army attire, a big army tank truck, and a huge round wooden barrel-like object. I tried to get closer to see them and see why they were there. I felt something was about to happen and in that moment the water started coming back toward us and it was coming back strong. I felt the sand beneath my feet starting to pull inward toward the ocean and I could see the water rising. I yelled to my husband, RUN! As I turned to start running, I could feel the powerful pull of the sand pulling me in toward the ocean and the water wave rising to the height of skyscrapers. It was coming and, in that moment, I knew there was no way we were going to outrun it. I felt the wave drop over us—we were engulfed by the ocean, and then I woke up.

THE TRUTH I KNOW NOW

At the time I wasn't sure what this meant. I thought it was a sign or warning that a war was coming to our country. It was indeed a war coming but it was a war for my soul. This wasn't a physical war—it was spiritual. When you open these doors there are prices to pay—you don't walk away scot-free. This was a call for war. The very next night I had another dream.

DREAM: THE SPIRAL STAIRCASE

I dreamt of a big body of water, a vast ocean. I was walking up an open spiral staircase with a body of water to my left and to my right was the hollow center of this open spiral staircase. There was grass and wooden objects below on the ground and a long fall from the height I was at on the staircase. The ocean felt a bit further off in the distance. My husband was on the step in front of me and there were five people I knew on the steps behind me, some work associates and some close friends. I turned slowly to look down and felt an intense fear of the height I was at. When turning back, I lost my balance, and I fell. I fell toward the center of the spiral stairs. When I fell, everyone fell with me, like we were connected somehow. Once I hit the ground, I saw my husband, as a child; I was holding him in my arms to console him as he spoke to me.

THE TRUTH I KNOW NOW

The Holy Spirit revealed to me that I am called to lead a people. And when I fall, they fall. When my destiny is delayed—whether from lack of knowledge or disobedience—I'm delaying a people's need. God's call and will for your life is not about *you*. It never has been: it's bigger than you. So do yourself a favor and get over yourself and out of your own way. Your fall is never your fall alone. We are one.

Matthew 7:13–14
"Enter through the narrow gate. For the gate is wide and the road broad that leads to destruction, and there are many who go through it. How narrow is the gate and difficult the road that leads to life, and few find it."

DREAM: LEVIATHAN AND GOD'S HAND

In this dream there was an indoor store, in a much bigger establishment, that people went to. I saw a guy while in this store that stood out to me, not sure why. He had one son and said he was lucky his wife didn't want any more because she didn't like kids. When I left this store, I realized I didn't have my phone and wasn't sure where my husband was, so I went back into the store and approached an Asian woman behind the counter. I asked if she could call my husband, she said, "yes," and as the phone rang, I realized I gave her my number. I didn't bother to say anything, I just thanked her and prepared myself to go find him. There was a big body of water to our left that I glanced at as I turned from the counter. She said, "do you know there are sea creatures in there?" She continued speaking: "people try to hide it but it's true I'll show you." We walked out of the shop onto a wooden dock-like platform, it felt like it was being held by buoys or something, it wasn't stable. She pointed to the left and I saw silver thick skin shining and moving around and I thought they are so small: it was just a group of fish. In that moment, my spirit was picking up on something to my right and as I looked over to my right, the woman was no longer on the platform with me and there to my right was a huge dark green serpent or dragon-like creature, with skin like leather, it moved very stealthily so that it went undetected. I knew in that moment it was a trap: she tried to deflect my attention to the left while that creature was on my right. When it realized I had seen it, it started to move through the water exposing more of its body. It was nothing I have ever seen before; it was ancient, and it was massive. When it moved, the entire body of water moved and made very strong waves. I was knocked off the dock and fell into the water, and as I fell into the water I was frozen with fear. All I could remember as I was falling was that there was a cage or barrier separating the bodies of water and I wasn't sure which side of the barrier I fell on. I was terrified, the ocean water was dark and deep. I remember opening my eyes under the water to see where it was, but there was sand and debris from the movement of this beast that stirred the bottom of the sea and obscured my view. In that moment of panic and fear, before I could scream for help, I was on a bed of smooth rocks, as if I had been lifted out of the water and washed ashore and I could hear a calm stream of water running over the rocks.

THE TRUTH I KNOW NOW

That was the Hand of God. I went from a moment of panic, fear, and chaos to calm, still water. God pulled me out of the water before I could finish screaming in fear. He showed me His hand in my life. If you recall, I was warned in the spirit during the Elemental Immersion retreat the night before the water ritual by the sound of a siren. The marine kingdom is not one to play with; it is vicious, and the depth of its evil is indescribable. Without God Almighty, you do not stand a chance.

Psalm 104:7–9
At your rebuke the water fled; at the sound of your thunder, they hurried away—mountains rose and valleys sank—to the place you established for them. You set a boundary they cannot cross; they will never cover the earth again.

Job 38:8–11
Who enclosed the sea behind doors when it burst from the womb, when I made the clouds its garment and total darkness its blanket, when I determined its boundaries and put its bars and doors in place, when I declared, "You may come this far, but no farther; your proud waves stop here?"

Job 41:1,9–10
Can you pull in Leviathan with a hook or tie his tongue down with a rope? Any hope of capturing him proves false. Does a person not collapse at the very sight of him? No one is ferocious enough to rouse Leviathan; who then can stand against me?

The Call for Deliverance

I connected with the woman whose testimony had pierced through the veil of deception in my life. Up until this point, my prayers were constant—asking God to show me where I had gone astray and reveal what I was doing wrong. And He did just that. When I spoke with her, I shared how her testimony had reached me, how my own experience mirrored parts of hers, and how shaken I felt after watching. We prayed together, we communed, and we gave God the glory for keeping me.

As we talked, she explained things that made sense. Then she asked about my throat. I froze. I didn't say a word. I waited. Why had my throat come up in every spiritual space I'd been in? The last had been during my conversation with Faith just a few months before. How were they privy to this information and why, I thought. It had also been a theme in many of my dreams. My throat has been very significant in my walk. I just wasn't clear on what it meant. I asked how she knew, and she smiled. I wasn't asking as if I knew, because I didn't. She then said, "your voice is a part of your gift" and "it is very significant on your walk with God."

Her words awakened many memories. I knew that to be true and there had been multiple attempts on my throat and they all started to rush back to the surface: the enemy's attempt to silence me and the attacks I couldn't explain. I began to see clearly for the first time how I was a threat to the enemy, how he was attacking me. And that my voice is what he fears. It wasn't until this moment that I started to see the bigger picture—how the enemy had been at work in my life and how every child of God is a threat to his schemes.

THE ENEMY'S ATTEMPTS TO SILENCE ME

The first attempt on my throat was physical. I was in my early twenties, living what I thought was my "best life" in Manhattan. At the time, I was in a long-term relationship with someone I believed was the one. We did everything together. One night, after hopping from one iconic lounge to another, we were walking back to the car to head home. Suddenly, I heard my name. I turned and saw my childhood friend. We ran to each other and hugged tight; it had been years. I invited her to come stay with us and we would hang out in the morning to catch up. Between the two of them I never stopped laughing; there was never a dull moment. When we got back to the apartment, she went to the guest room. My significant other, at that time, and I stayed up talking, but our conversation turned into a disagreement. And without warning, his hands were around my neck. Darkness.

When I came back to consciousness, it took a moment for my vision to focus. I saw him hovering over me, his face filled with terror—terror I had never seen in him before. His body shook as if he himself couldn't comprehend what had just happened. When I fully realized it, I thanked God that I was alive.

Then his phone rang. It was 3 a.m. On the other end was a woman's voice. Her first words: "Is she okay?" "Yes," he replied. "There is another spirit in the house—a woman," she said. The woman that called was not just anyone. She had been with him since birth, a spiritual figure revered in his culture, one he had told me about before but that I had dismissed as unusual, mysterious. In his culture, it was normal to have a birth attendant, but I had never understood the weight of it.

What I didn't know then was that this was not just cultural. This was spiritual.

Dream: Throat Being Slit

This night I had many micro dreams in one. Most were at a retreat-like setting with many people in attendance, and the overall feeling of the dream was strange. Lots of people hiding behind masks, not literally, it was people not being authentic. I was cut in the neck by a man with scissors so that I couldn't speak my truth. He didn't cut deep enough though, so it took a long time for me to die. I was able to tell a girl (the girl resembled my oldest niece) what happened and to leave the place we were at. I woke up at exactly 3:33 a.m.

Dream: Flash of Black and the Man That Held Me

Many parts to the dream. I was attending a sports event, there were competitions involving swimming and candy shops. When I returned to my hotel, I walked through the door and dropped my things. As I walked to my bedroom, I saw a flash of black in my peripheral view. In that moment a woman attacked me: she was hiding behind my bedroom door. My spirit knew someone was there and that they were there to try to hurt me. She attacked me and we fell on the bed. She grabbed for my throat, but I put my foot on her neck to choke her and get her grip off me. The most liberating and memorable part of this dream was a man that appeared: he held me like I was a child and sang or hummed the most angelic song or hymn I've ever heard. He said, *"Do you remember; sing it with me, all will be okay."* I felt so safe and deeply calm in his arms. The embrace felt familiar like I knew him, but I didn't recognize his face his arms were brown.

Joshua 10:24–25

"Come near and put your feet on the necks of these kings." And they came near, and put their feet upon the necks of them. And Joshua said to them, Fear not, nor be dismayed. Be strong and courageous, for the LORD will do this to all the enemies you fight.

Dream: Very Tall Entity

In this dream I was with a close childhood friend, and she was talking to me, so my guard was down. We were both lying down when I turned and saw a dark spirit standing over me. He was very tall: he towered over me, and I could see his face, it was very fair and pale. I became fearful and I knew he was going to try and harm me. When I tried to move, he put his hands around my neck to choke me and I woke.

Back to the Call

The closer I drew near, the closer I came to truly walking with Jesus Christ and building a stronger relationship with Him, the stronger the enemy's attacks became. I knew at this point that I was moving in the right direction. The resistance grew heavier, and I could sense that this force didn't like it and didn't want me to get wherever this path was leading me. I now recognize it as one of the enemy's strategies to keep me from stepping fully into my calling.

I shared a few of my dreams with her, including the one about the army in the water. She explained that they were marine spirits. I had never heard the term before—I wrote it down to research later. Then she said something that pierced me: "You have many gifts God has given you; you've just been growing them under the wrong covenant."

We prayed again, and she encouraged me to fast for seven days. We scheduled a deliverance call following the fast. Deliverance—another word I wrote down. I was an infant in Christ during this time. But I was seeking Him, and I was seeking Him with all my heart. She also mentioned a hundred-day prayer challenge she was leading for the community—about halfway through at the time—and invited me to join. She told me to remove all objects that are not of God from my home. As she said this, my mind went to all the crystals and spiritual items I had accumulated. I didn't care. After the call, I went through the house like it was trash day, and I had to make it before the garbage man came.

After the call, I prayed again—asking God to watch over me, protect me, and to allow only what is in His will for my life. I felt her to be genuine but at this point in my life, I wasn't taking anything for face value. It needed to go through and be confirmed by God.

I decided to request the link for the prayer challenge and planned to start the seven-day fast at the beginning of the week.

Around that time, I noticed she had a Christian mentorship with limited spots available. The announcement stated that, because of the depth of the material and the personal attention required, only a few people would be selected and notified via email. I didn't know exactly what it entailed, and how it would be. I'd never done any type of mentorship, but I figured if there was any mentoring I needed at this time in my life, this would be it. I signed up and left it to God.

During this time of my life, I wasn't sure where to start in the Bible, so I decided to read one Psalm a day. I had already built a routine of praying and reading first thing in the morning. I had been consistent. But on this particular morning, I felt prompted to go deeper—to spend more time. My spirit was feeling uneasy, full of questions. I remember asking God one of the most common questions: *I'm calling out to you God, where are you?* I asked Him to help me find my way back home.

That day I landed on Psalm 23. When I reached the words, "He lets me lie down in green pastures," it took me back to my experience in the Reiki class. Right then, God reminded me that He had never left me—not then, and not now. In my notes, I had also written down Psalm 71. I didn't want to skip ahead in Scripture, but I also didn't know why or when I had written it down. But I felt the nudge to read it. When I read it, I smiled with teary eyes. It was everything I needed in this moment. How beautifully God works.

The Call for Deliverance

Psalm 71:1–6

Lord, I seek refuge in you; let me never be disgraced. In your justice, rescue and deliver me; listen closely to me and save me. Be a rock of refuge for me, where I can always go. Give the command to save me, for you are my rock and fortress. Deliver me, my God from the power of the wicked, from the grasp of the unjust and oppressive. For you are my hope, Lord God, my confidence from my youth. I have leaned on you from birth; you took me from my mother's womb.

Cleaning House: Getting My House in Order

I woke up with yesterday still heavy on my mind. I wanted to learn more, to understand, and to better equip myself and my family. But the first thing I felt was anger. The deceit and evil within the very things I once thought were pure—it was deeply disturbing.

I said my morning prayer, then went downstairs for round two of cleaning house. Anything that resembled a lie, anything questionable or "on the fence," went straight in the trash. As I cleared things out, I spoke aloud prayers over my home. On my way upstairs, I caught a glimpse of myself in the entryway mirror. My face was set with anger. I was angry. Angry that I had been misled. Angry at the thought that so many people were still entangled, maybe not even realizing the depths of deception they were in.

When I reached the ancestral altar, it was harder. I had poured love into "taking care" of my elevated ancestors. I packed it all up into a garbage bag and out the door it went. In my peripheral vision I could see my husband watching. He probably thought I had lost my mind. I could see him trying to grab things from my sight, moving them out of the path of destruction. I remember him saying how much money was being thrown away. I knew it was hard for him to see, but that didn't stop me. None of it mattered. None of it was worth my soul. I kept going. When I finished, I sat in silence. I repented. I opened Scripture and prayed over my home. Tears flowed. I released it all. Then I made myself some coffee and tried to start my day.

But I didn't feel good, and I didn't want to push through the day. A heaviness weighed on me. I felt down. Sad. Lost. Just days earlier I had been full of life, convinced I was finally on the right track, finally on my way back. But now? I was struggling. Instead of fighting the feeling, I lay down and let it be. I put on some gospel music and closed my eyes.

When I got up, a sermon appeared on my feed. I wasn't one to follow preachers or content in this way—the algorithms were at work, for sure. Later that day, I was introduced to Billy Graham on my feed—which I enjoyed. But this one looked to be an old sermon from many years ago from Bishop Jakes. Now before you start judging—don't. In that moment of my life, the message he gave was exactly what I needed. Remember, God used Judas to fulfill prophecy. Not comparing him to Judas in any way, but I believe once anointed doesn't mean always anointed—it is a blessing that must be stewarded. He and he alone, like anyone, will have to answer to God. In this moment he delivered the Word.

Up to this point, I had never watched any sermons before

that I can recall, so I wondered why this one came. I was and still am very intentional that my focus remains on God, following His voice and learning His ways, not man's. But in that moment this message pierced straight to my soul. The heart of his message was this: sometimes God places us in Adullam so we can discover who we are apart from everyone else. It's where you learn that you are still chosen, still anointed, even when you don't yet see the Kingdom. Adullam is where God heals you, rebuilds your courage, and prepares you to carry the weight of what's next. Those words met me right where I was. I was seen, understood, and most importantly, God was reminding me that my present place was not my final destination. What stuck with me most was this: your discontentment is there to draw you out into exceptionalism. It will drive you into your destiny.

DREAM: WHEN GOD SAID ENOUGH

I was going down rivers, many different rivers big and small. There were many turns and branches of rivers. The ship was tall and slim, it was some type of party ship; I saw a broadcasting news symbol on the side of the ship. There were Asians cooking and or managing parts of the ship. There were a few people that I knew from grade school onboard. As the ship started on its journey all seemed okay, we were calmly moving down the river canal. I remember looking around and it didn't look like our reality anymore. I was standing on the deck, looking at our surroundings, and it looked like we entered an ancient time. At one of the riverbeds, we made a sharp right turn and started to speed down another river canal. In this moment I knew this had been a trap, it wasn't the ship it advertised to be. I remember looking around as we sped down this river to see if I knew where we were and where we were heading. I could see other adjacent rivers: this was an ancient place. Suddenly, we started to spin: the entire ship started to spin, counterclockwise, I could hear everyone on board being tossed and the sound of panic. We were crashing, as we were spinning, knocking into land and everything around it. It was chaos; we were spinning in chaos. As we were in mid-spin a Lion appeared standing firmly on the land, in a visible distance: majestically and with great power, where the ship was heading to crash, and the ship came to a complete abrupt halt!

THE TRUTH I KNOW NOW

Jesus came for me, and He protected me. My God the LORD of armies, LORD of hosts, when He acts, who can reverse it.

Genesis 49:10
The scepter will not depart from Judah or the staff from between his feet until He whose right it is comes; and to Him shall be the obedience of the people.

2 Timothy 4:16–17
At my first defense, no one stood by me, but everyone deserted me. May it not be counted against them. But the LORD stood with me and strengthened me, so that

I might fully preach the word, and all the Gentiles might hear it.

The night before this dream Psalm 69 was the Scripture we prayed in the community prayer session:

Psalm 69:1–5,15–18

Save me, God, for the water has risen to my neck. I have sunk in deep mud, and there is no footing; I have come into deep water, and a flood sweeps over me. I am weary from my crying; my throat is parched. My eyes fail, looking for my God. Those who hate me without cause are more numerous than the hairs on my head; my deceitful enemies, who would destroy me, are powerful. Though I did not steal, I must repay. God, you know my foolishness, and my guilty acts are not hidden from you.

Don't let the floodwaters sweep over me or the deep swallow me up; don't let the Pit close its mouth over me. Answer me, LORD, for your faithful love is good in keeping with your abundant compassion, turn to me. Don't hide your face from your servant, for I am in distress. Answer me quickly! Come near to me and redeem me; ransom me because of my enemies.

I have no words for His timing and power. My God came to my rescue and prepared me the night before this dream. Though I saw the battle between forces for my soul, He allowed me to see that He is in control and that the victory is already won. "Although I walk through the valley of the shadow of death, I will fear no evil, for thou art with me."

Marriage: Unequal Yoking

"*If you follow an unbeliever long enough, their way of life will become your way of life.*" When you live outside of God's will, it touches every area of your life—marriage included. As I returned home to God, I quickly learned the weight of being unequally yoked. And, as with so many other lessons, I learned the hard way.

When I started "running" after God, everything shifted. Suddenly I was met with resistance. At first, it felt strange and confusing, but then it became clear—this was a spiritual battle. Everything was fine when I was going the wrong way. When I was living apart from God, living in my own way and following my own will—I wasn't a threat to the enemy then, I was a companion. I was unknowingly on his side. But once I made the conscious decision and turned toward God, all you know what broke loose. The attacks grew sharper, and one of the greatest battlegrounds was within my marriage. If you pay attention, the enemy reveals himself and where he is at work in your life every time. At this point he was working through my marriage.

My husband is a good man with a kind and genuine heart. But the enemy will use anyone and anything to get to you—especially when he has legal access. Culturally and religiously, we come from different worlds. Out of love for him—and for his soul—I tried to share what I had seen and known in the Spirit. While trying to maintain respect for his beliefs, I thought,

"Who am I to sway him from what he believes?", but my concerns for him grew. God had been working on me so much, it came to a point where whether I wanted to or not it would just pour out, I was full of the Word. I wanted everyone to know Him, to experience Him. But I learned quickly that this is God's work, not mine. If it is His will, He will move. Still, that didn't change the reality I was facing: the misalignment was real, and I was living the consequences of my choices.

This day I was met with the painful reality of just how much I was in misalignment and the mess I had gotten myself in. I got a reminder text that it was the Festival of Lights that day, a holiday celebrated in his culture. This had been the first since I had started my run back to God. I was completely unprepared for how I would navigate it. They didn't know this woman—the one I was becoming. I felt like I needed to reintroduce myself. The woman who was once easygoing, open, and accepting was now intentional, purposeful, and burning with a fervent heart for the Lord. Playtime was over. Before I had the chance to explain that I would no longer partake in their religious practices, one of the most significant events arrived that very day. And I had no choice but to face it.

Before getting out of bed, I prayed—asking God for His protection while I was there, and for wisdom on how to move forward in a way that wound not cause offense. I told my husband where I stood: I would not partake in the readings or worship of their religious practices. He responded by saying that this particular holiday was good, that there was beauty in its meaning—that its purpose was to bring light into the darkness of the world. At this point in my walk, I was willing to listen, that's only fair. But even after hearing him out, I remained firm in my conviction and stood for what I said.

Later, I went down to feed Savannah. As I watered my plants in the kitchen, a bird flew in front of me—it was a hawk. I recognized it immediately from the speckled markings on its body. Curious, and during this time still leaning on the search engine, I looked up the biblical significance of the hawk (as stated on hymnsandverses.com):

- **A reminder of God's guidance:** Just as hawks in the Bible symbolize divine guidance, seeing a hawk today may serve as a reminder that God is watching over us and directing our paths.
- **A call to develop spiritual vision:** The keen eyesight of the hawk can be a reminder for us to cultivate our spiritual vision, seeking wisdom and discernment from above.
- **A symbol of strength and power:** The powerful hunting abilities of the hawk can inspire us to face our challenges with courage and determination, trusting in God's strength to see us through.[1]

In that moment, I knew—it was not coincidence. I was covered and His plan is much bigger than me. A call to walk in obedience even when you don't understand it. God never fails!

---

1 https://hymnsandverses.com/biblical-meaning-of-seeing-a-hawk/

Job 39:26–28 (NKJV)
Do the hawk fly by your wisdom, and spread its wings toward the south? Does the eagle mount up at your command, and make its nest on high? On the rock it dwells and resides, on the crag of the rock and the stronghold.

In this passage, God speaks to Job as a reminder of His role as the Creator: of His omnipotence and the majesty of His wisdom. Through rhetorical questions, God calls Job and all believers to trust His plan, especially in times of questioning, uncertainty, and struggle. It is a call not to lean on our own understanding but to acknowledge Him in all we do.

Isaiah 46:11 (NIV)
"From the east I summon a bird of prey; from a far-off land, a man to fulfill my purpose. What I have said that I will bring about; what I have planned, that I will do."

In this verse, God uses the metaphor of a bird of prey to represent a powerful instrument through which He will use to execute His plans and accomplish His purpose. The bird of prey symbolizes swiftness, determination, and strength. I was blown away and knew in this moment to trust God, He is in control.

That same day's Scripture was **Psalm 32**, a passage centered on the reflection and blessing of divine forgiveness. I find it so amazing, many times I sit in awe, at how perfectly everything aligned—my private study, the prayer challenge community, and now the unexpected sign of the hawk. In this moment of my life, the timing was too precious to ignore. Only God could orchestrate in this way, with such precision.

Psalm 32:7-8 (NKJV)
You are my hiding place; You shall preserve me from trouble; You shall surround me with songs of deliverance. Selah. I will instruct you and teach you in the way you should go; I will guide you with My eye.

That morning, I was praising God for His grace and mercy—so beautiful, especially considering how often I had once lived in ways that went against His will. Just the night before, I had prayed in the shower, pouring out my heart. I had prayed over my marriage, and our life at this point, asking God if it was His will to help us through it, and if not, show me the way. I prayed about my career; though I was well-compensated, it was more important for me to be in full alignment with God. I was unfulfilled. I knew I was missing the mark—missing His purpose for my life, with the noise and pointless accomplishments. They meant nothing at this point. Some might call it crazy or ungrateful to step away from success; I say, call me what you want. I can testify that gaining everything can feel like nothing. It is the emptiest space I have ever known. The last thing I wanted in this moment was to repeat a cycle of delay. My prayer was simple: *Your will be done in my life. No more delay, Abba.*

Back to the Challenge

As my husband reminded me, this holiday is collectively a day celebrated to symbolize the victory of light over darkness and knowledge over ignorance. I had once loved it for that reason. During that time, I believed it did stand for a good cause from a conceptual perspective. But in practice, the version I was exposed to involved puja—prayers and offerings to deities. This was where I had to draw the line. I told my husband I could not partake in the puja, or reading the stories. His reply was sharp: "Then you shouldn't come."

I knew he was upset, and honestly, I understood. Our marriage was already in a fragile state, and this only added more shaking. But instead of reacting, I accepted his words with peace. "Okay, I'll stay," I said gently. I meant it—I wanted to use this time for more reading anyway. And in my spirit, I asked the Holy Spirit to guide me as I began researching the holiday more deeply.

1 Peter 4:12–17

Dear friends, don't be surprised when the fiery ordeal comes among you to test you, as if something unusual were happening to you. Instead, rejoice as you share in the sufferings of Christ, so that you may also rejoice with great joy when his glory is revealed. If you are ridiculed for the name of Christ, you are blessed, because the Spirit of glory and of God rests on you. Let none of you suffer as a murderer, a thief, an evildoer, or a meddler. But if anyone suffers as a Christian, let him not be ashamed but let him glorify God in having that name. For the time has come for judgment to begin with God's household, and if it begins with us, what will the outcome be for those who disobey the gospel of God?

Later, my husband came back into my office and said, "Hinduism is the oldest religion in the world. Christianity is one of the newest created." I paused. It seemed we were both at that time researching our views, trying to make sense of things from where we each stood. I replied "Yes, I see, that's interesting"; I wasn't sure of his point. I thought, *Well, there would be no Christians without Christ. He came at an appointed time for an appointed purpose so why would it be older than His time.* During this time of my life, I felt the urge to defend my faith, and I'm sure it was what we were both wanting to do. But I didn't want to argue. What I did know was simple: whether Christianity was the oldest or the youngest religion it didn't matter to me. I serve one God, the living God—and that wasn't changing.

Not after how far I had fallen away from Him, and certainly not now that I was running back. Nothing was going to come between that again. Absolutely nothing. I realized from that moment forward, I had to be intentional, vigilant, and clear about what I gave my time, attention, and acceptance to. This was no longer about debate; it was about obedience.

I needed my feet on solid ground. I wasn't angry with him, nor was I trying to argue or force a change in his beliefs. I could only walk in my own journey and share what the Holy Spirit had revealed to me. I knew this was difficult for him—the old me had been there with him for everything. But this version of me was different.

Not long after, he came back into my office a third time and said, "You can come." I had to laugh, because I never asked permission or had the desire to. Of course, this was his way of asking me to join, but I was no longer playing the game: no more tug-of-war with my convictions. I had already checked out. I was no longer looking for answers or opinions from people. Instead, I thought back to what God already spoke to me: remember His role as Creator and trust His plan. I opened my Bible and landed on John 16:12–15. The Scripture was red, and it read:

John 16:12–14 (KJV)
I have yet many things to say to you, but you cannot bear them now. However, when He, the Spirit of truth, has come, He will guide you into all truth: for He will not speak on his own authority, but whatever He hears He will speak; and He will tell you things to come. He will glorify Me, for He will take of what is Mine and declare it to you.

In this moment I understood this passage on many levels; I cannot judge or condemn anyone according to their beliefs. I can only remain obedient in my walk and have compassion as everyone navigates through life. I can only speak for what the Holy Spirit has been and has shown me in my life—God's will *will be done*.

After reading this passage, I paused. Every part of me wanted to share it with my husband, but I held back. I knew he wouldn't understand—or worse, he would downplay it as a coincidence to try to make logical sense of it. God will not be mocked, and at that point in my walk, I could no longer tolerate his mockery. Life and death are in the power of the tongue. I knew then that I was covered. Secure in that, I told him I would go to support him.

On the ride to the house, I tried to share my testimony hoping he might then understand my sternness, my stance, and my heart as his wife. Up until now, I had gone through and carried all of this in solitude. During those seasons of my life, I felt it was unfair—how I had been walking through so many changes and challenges without the emotional and conversational support of my husband, or anyone, really. But the truth I know now is: I was exactly where God wanted me. He has always been my comfort, my strength, my Source. All I had to do was learn to trust Him.

I don't believe this was deliberate from the people in my life, by any means. My husband loves and adores me as do the people in my life. This is a spiritual thing. This entire journey I've walked alone in the physical, but my spirit has always been held and guided. There would be times I would try to share, and the words would not come to me. I never forced it; not everyone has spiritual knowledge. The people closest to me felt the farthest away, and the ones who had promised to always be there were gone. As time passed, and as I grew in Him, I knew He had me right where He wanted me.

THE TRUTH I KNOW NOW

Galatians 1:1
Paul, an apostle: not from men or by man but by Jesus Christ and God the Father who raised him from the dead.

1 Corinthians 2:12–15

Now we have not received the spirit of the world, but the Spirit who comes from God, so that we may understand what has been freely given to us by God. We also speak these things, not in words taught by human wisdom, but in those taught by Spirit, explaining spiritual things to spiritual people. But the person without the Spirit does not receive what comes from God's Spirit, because it is foolishness to him; he is not able to understand it since it is evaluated spiritually. The spiritual person, however, can evaluate everything, and yet he himself cannot be evaluated by anyone.

Isaiah 41:10

Do not fear, for I am with you; do not be afraid, for I am your God. I will strengthen you; I will help you; I will hold on to you with my righteous right hand.

2 Timothy 4:16

At my first defense, no one stood by me, but everyone deserted me. May it not be counted against them. But the LORD stood with me and strengthened me, so that I might fully preach the word, and all the Gentiles might hear it.

We made it to my father-in-law's house. Being there has always been hard for me—not because of the people, but because of the battle I could sense behind the scenes. I could see the good in them, even as I knew the enemy used them. Even knowing that in their hearts they had once cursed me, I still loved them.

He cooked so much food, and we enjoyed a good time together. The neighbors joined us with their children, and laughter filled the house. But when it came time for puja, my spirit grew heavy. Quietly, I prayed. I prayed that God Almighty would bring them truth. I whispered, "Jesus Christ is the light of the world, a light no darkness can penetrate. YHWH is the one and only—God of all gods, King of all kings, Lord of all lords, Alpha and Omega, Creator of heaven and earth, Beginning and the End." I prayed that He would open their eyes and touch their hearts, if it was in His will. That night when we returned home, I told my husband what I had prayed during puja. He laughed and thought I had lost my mind. But I was never more sound.

SEVEN-DAY FAST

The next morning marked the first day of my fast. It was the first time in my life I've ever fasted on purpose. I woke up tired—my alarm when off at 5:30 a.m., and I hit snooze. But when it alarmed the second time, my eyes flew open, and a sudden surge of energy jolted me out of bed. It startled me. I jumped to my feet and went straight to my office to begin my day in prayer and worship. After prayer, I returned to Psalm 32 and read it again. It was such a timely Word—still speaking directly into my situation. I reflected, prayed through it, and gave thanks for where God had me and for the work He was doing in my life.

As I was getting into the rhythm of my day, adjusting without my morning coffee, I noticed that on this day, of all days, my husband had decided to wake up early. My husband is not a morning person. Not only did he wake up early—he cooked breakfast. We had been together at this point for nine years, and I could count on one hand how many times either of these things have occurred in our relationship. To top it off, he even came into my office with his plate and asked if I was hungry. Before I could respond, he followed up—half rhetorical, half mocking—with, "So you can't have coffee either?"

I stayed silent. Some things do not deserve a response. As he walked back upstairs, he sipped his coffee loudly and voiced his satisfaction in a way that was impossible to miss. He knew today was my first day of fasting. One thing I realized in that moment was God had brought me a long way from who I used to be—and I was grateful. I prayed. I asked God to continue to show me the way. Deep down, I knew that this too was spiritual.

Trust Him

By this time, I had completed my seven-day fast. I had some catch-up reading to do and was on Psalm 39 that day. It was also the day of my scheduled deliverance call, and I was looking forward to it. I got up early, said my prayers, and prepared for the day. However, I didn't have a meeting link in my inbox, so I reached out to check in. She informed me she had mistakenly double-booked, apologized, and asked if we could reschedule for the next day—same time. Schedule-wise, I was fine, but I had been genuinely anticipating my deliverance. I reminded myself: *It's all good; I'll be ready tomorrow, bright and early.*

That evening, during the community prayer challenge session, we were on Psalm 78. It is a very long passage covering lessons from Israel's past, God's wrath and mercy among His people, and the importance of trusting Him. I took many notes that resonated deeply with me:

- Have trust and faith in the Lord. God does not like when we doubt. Don't forget what He has done when you are faced with a new challenge in your life.
- He is the same God now as He was then.
- Trust: this is one thing He truly wants from his children and waits for.
- Repent for the times you have questioned Him and never came to Him for your problems and challenges. And the times you didn't give Him the rightful praise.

- God takes lineages into account. Those in His covenant who pray and are faithful to Him are blessed across generations. (I thanked God for my father's relationship with Him, because I know that has held me and kept me safe.)
- Don't limit Him with your own understanding.
- Trust Him completely and to show me the areas where I struggle with this.

Things that came to mind to repent for when writing this note that I jotted down in that moment to take into prayer later:

- Not being still and truly trusting where you are taking me.
- To thank Him for keeping me through it all.

In the center of the page, I wrote the biggest reminder for myself:

TRUST HIM

The next morning, I woke up early ready to start the day and prepare for the rescheduled deliverance call. I was a little tired, but I paused to catch the sunrise from my bedroom window. After taking a shower and getting ready, I centered myself in prayer, lifting my head to the sky. I thanked God for His grace and asked for guidance in living this new life with Him, and for the ability to share His greatness. It was getting close to the scheduled time for the call and I felt a nudge by the Holy Spirit to open my Bible and read my next Psalm chapter for the day before starting my day. It was Psalm 40: I cried deeply.

Psalm 40:1–8, 11–14

I waited patiently for the Lord, and he turned to me and heard my cry for help. He brought me up from a desolate pit, out of the miry clay, and set my feet on a rock, making my steps secure. He put a new song in my mouth, a hymn of praise to our God. Many will see and fear, and they will trust in the Lord. Blessed is the man who has put his trust in the Lord and has not turned to the proud or to those who run after lies. Lord my God, you have done many things—your wondrous works and your plans for us; none can compare with you. If I were to report and speak of them, they are more than can be told. Then I said, "See, I have come; in the scroll it is written about me. I delight to do your will, my God, and your instruction is deep within me." Lord, you do not withhold your compassion from me. Your constant love and truth will always guard me. For troubles without number have surrounded me; my iniquities have overtaken me; I am unable to see. They are more than the hairs of my head, and my courage leaves me. Lord, be pleased to rescue me; hurry to help me, Lord. Let those who intend to take my life be disgraced and confounded. Let those who wish me harm be turned back and humiliated. You are my helper and deliverer; my God, do not delay.

I could not control my tears. I stayed right there weeping in His presence. God's timing is unmatched and divinely orchestrated. He shows me time and time again who He is. I prayed that I never forget these moments. I thought: *God had heard my cry and my call. My God is living, He is worthy, and He is faithful!* I dried my eyes and hurried to get on the meeting call. I couldn't wait to share this experience with her after my deliverance. When I logged on, my camera wasn't working again. I thought, *Here we go.* I emailed to let her know I would restart my laptop and be right back. The restart worked, now it's about ten minutes after our scheduled time. I was online, but still waiting to be let in the meeting room. The meeting was still pending the host; no one showed, no emails received. I felt this to be strange—didn't seem like her. I emailed again—crickets. I waited in the meeting room until it kicked me out, twice.

My mind started racing with thoughts. I emailed her one more time, then paused, sensing that something else was happening. Perhaps something had happened to her. I prayed for her and sent one last message. Then I stopped, logged off: I asked the Holy Spirit what was happening, why was this happening? I closed my laptop and just listened.

The thoughts trying to creep in were not from God. It was the enemy's attempt to deceive me, by tempting me to think I needed someone outside of God to deliver me. Old traumas of abandonment and other memories surfaced. I could see the enemy's angle, but in that moment, I chose God. I had a knowing, God was speaking, and I was missing the entire lesson here. Being so fixated on something outside myself. The Holy Spirit reminded me of that morning's Scripture, Psalm 40: *That He has heard my cry, and He has delivered me*—period.

He even prepared me the night before to TRUST HIM completely. You can search this entire universe; you will never find a love like God's.

Side Note

The greatest gift in writing this book has been revisiting these notes, journal entries, and recordings, watching it all come together—and witnessing God's work firsthand. How He has been so strategic and intentional in my life, every detail. Some parts were tough, seeing how vulnerable and naïve I once was. And then there are moments like this, where my short-term memory failed me: I remember early on while writing this book, I came back to this very entry, and I was so hard on myself. Only after I told myself, *didn't you just write "TRUST HIM" in your notes the night before? How much louder do you need Him to be?*—did I fall back to sleep.

But the truth is that we as a people are so programed to believe it is something or someone outside of us that must help us, that we shift the responsibility on someone or something else. The walk with God is certainly not easy but it is yours to bear. No one else can do it for you, no one else can save you. You can't ride on someone else's faith. God wants you, not a representative. He doesn't need an interpreter. He taught me years of lessons in this single moment. He is in the detail of our lives; you just have to quiet down. Seek Him, listen and pay attention.

Back to the Story

I asked myself why on earth was I placing this much trust and control in another person for my salvation—even writing this now blows my mind. We are not talking about a Bible study call—this is your soul. Did I not learn from my first lesson? I know one thing—I learned this day. I praised Him and cried out with joy. In that moment I heard the Holy Spirit clearly: *Trust Me, not man. Trust Me.* I cried uncontrollably and praised Him more. My God! I pray you hear me when I say, do not seek in any man what only God can do.

Ephesians 2:8–9
For you are saved by grace through faith, and this is not from yourselves; it is God's gift—not from works, so that no one can boast.

John 14:6–7
Jesus told him, "I am the way, the truth, and the life. No one comes to the Father except through me. If you know me, you will also know my Father."

Psalm 18:1–6
I love you, Lord, my strength. The Lord is my rock, my fortress, and my deliverer, my God, my rock where I seek refuge, my shield and the horn of my salvation, my stronghold. I called to the Lord, who is worthy of praise, and I was saved from my enemies. The ropes of death were wrapped around me; the torrents of destruction terrified me. The ropes of Sheol

entangled me; the snares of death confronted me. I called to the
Lord in my distress, and I cried to my God for help. From his
temple he heard my voice, and my cry to him reached his ears.

I never rescheduled that call. I was delivered that morning. The best way I can describe that moment is a freeing—a release—a profound love and knowing that God has the final say. Trust Him. And when you seek Him with all your heart and soul, you will find Him. There was a lesson here and I received it. But spiritual deliverance is only the first step; God delivers us to lead us. It takes faith to believe and a surrendering to His will. What an amazing God we serve. It's His turn; He's waited so long.

Two detrimental mistakes that the Holy Spirit has revealed to me so far on this journey: first, the moment I started looking outside of myself for answers and direction, I was going the wrong way. The Kingdom of God is within His people. Second, I placed people over God's intended positions in my life without first testing their spirit—without confirming that they carried the heart of God within them.

Yes, I was delivered that day, but that didn't mean all was clear and that I was out of the woods, or that it would be smooth sailing from there. No, no—it was quite the opposite. God delivers us to lead us. Much like the Israelites in the wilderness, they had to learn how to inherit the Promised Land. There is much unlearning that needed to happen. They had been oppressed and enslaved to sin for so long that they had to learn God's way—how to walk as sons and daughters of the Most High. So, what did God do? He took them the long way home.

Exodus 13:17–18

When Pharaoh let the people go, God did not lead them along the road to the land of the Philistines, even though it was nearby; for God said, "The people will change their minds and return to Egypt if they face war." So he led the people around toward the Red Sea along the road of the wilderness. And the Israelites left the land of Egypt in battle formation.

I continued with my day, oblivious to the long journey ahead—the trials and tribulations that were sure to come on my walk with Christ. In my infancy in Him, I still had so much to learn. That day, I was doing research on the adversary—how he moves and how he deceives so many. Two particular points (on Wikipedia) caught my attention and brought to mind a dream I had a few months earlier:

- *Satan* (Hebrew) "Lord of the Inferno": The adversary, representing opposition, the element of fire, the direction of the south, and the Sigil of Baphomet during ritual.
- *Lucifer* (Latin) "The Morning Star": The bringer of light, representing pride and enlightenment, the element of air, the direction of the east, and candles during ritual.[2]

The phrase "bringer of light" caught my attention. I flipped back through my notes of past dreams—and there he was, Lucas, the "bringer of light."

---

2   https://en.wikipedia.org/wiki/Classification_of_demons.

Dream: Lucas, "Bringer of Light"

I was traveling in the dream, but it was within a similar area. The place I was at was like an apartment complex and an outdoorsy-styled motel-type complex. It was called Lucas. There was an outdoor live band that played at night. Seeing the stage and band equipment gave me an epiphany in the dream: in that moment I recalled a memory of people going to this place and posting pics about it. I was going between two places or worlds it felt like. It was like I was in some type of limbo, a middle ground, trying to understand or have enough courage to take the next step/direction in my life.

When I woke, I looked up the meaning of Lucas:

Lucas: Bringer of light. The name Lucas is the Latin form of the Greek name, and it means "bringer of light." Since Biblical times, Lucas and its variations have been used as a first name.

THE TRUTH I KNOW NOW

Without God's protection I would have never made it.

> Isaiah 14:12–17
> Shining morning star, how you have fallen from the heavens! You destroyer of nations, you have been cut down to the ground. You said to yourself, "I will ascend to the heavens, I will set up my throne above the stars of God. I will sit on the mount of the gods

assembly, in the remotest parts of the North. I will ascend above the highest clouds; I will make myself like the Most High. But you will be brought down to Sheol into the deepest regions of the Pit." Those who see you will stare at you; they will look closely at you: "Is this the man who caused the earth to tremble, who shook the kingdoms, who turned the world into a wilderness, who destroyed its cities and would not release the prisoners to return home?"

My Wrestle with God

Much like the Israelites when being freed from Pharoah's oppression, God did not take them into the Promised Land the very next day. There was time needed for unlearning and reprogramming from the years of captivity: they were a hot mess, as was I. The Israelites were not ready for the promise in the state of mind they were in. A purification process was necessary to strip away the fleshly things that were not of God. My own journey—coming in and out of the wilderness—was not easy. God works from the inside out, and that refining process can feel crushing on many levels.

One day, while listening to a community prayer session, I felt myself growing frustrated. The speaker talked about delays and blockages—how the enemy tries to derail you, distract you, and keep you from your blessing. I started to have an internal dialogue with God. I asked Him, almost angrily: "Why? Why drag us through torment. You're all-knowing. Why is it so hard to live in Your Word and follow You? How are we supposed to balance all of this with real life—with work, family and everything else? There seem to be endless 'watchouts': do this, don't do that, watch out the enemy will steal, and you have to make sure he doesn't, and on and on. And all these things to block us from You? You are God. Nothing should have the power to intercede a gift or blessing that You ordain, unless You allow it" … I paused. "Unless You allow it" lingered with me.

Her words broke through my pause: "If you don't have

someone in God to talk through your dreams with for guidance and understanding, ask the Holy Spirit to help you. Many times, your answers are in your dreams—but know it may take weeks, even twenty-one days, like Daniel." That was it, I was done. That statement sent me right back to my dialogue with God. I was furious. I have many dreams and visions—vivid, overwhelming dreams, and during this time was buried in them. How could I possibly wait weeks or months for the meaning of just one? You see, I wasn't chasing answers for entertainment. I was under spiritual attack. I was going to war in my sleep, and I didn't feel equipped to fight back. I was feeling alone and defeated. My rant turned into another dialogue of asking God "why?" In my desperation, I went back to my dreams, flipping through notes and old entries, trying to see where I had missed something—asking myself if God had truly been with me as His Word promises.

Then I stumbled across a dream I had recorded just the day before. I had completely forgotten it until I read it again—and when I did, it crushed me.

DREAM: GOD'S VOICE IN MY STORM

I was at the ocean, and massive waves and water were crashing past the shoreline. The tides were powerful, pulling everything in their path back into the depths of the ocean. I ran to grab one last thing, and I was pulled out by the water. I clung to a large rock to keep from being pulled under. I knew I didn't have much time before another wave would return. The crater I was in seemed impossible to climb out of, so I held tight to the rock.

Looking around, I saw that the surrounding craters were deep, and I screamed for help. From above and all around me, a voice spoke: "You are the cause of your own sorrow and drowning."

THE TRUTH I KNOW NOW

To the person reading this, I know—you don't have to say it. Trust me, I know. But at that time in my life, I was in darkness. I could not see, and I wasn't anchored in Him enough to recognize His voice. God was speaking to me. He was speaking as a Father, and every word He said was true. Looking back on this dream, remembering the place I was before fully walking with Him, I wept tears of joy, overwhelmed by His love. Our God is so good.

Deuteronomy 32:18
You ignored the Rock who gave you birth; you forgot the God who gave birth to you.

Psalm 18:31
For who is God besides the LORD? And who is a rock? Only our God.

There was a deeper lesson God revealed to me afterward. He brought to mind the story of Lot's wife and the destruction of Sodom and Gomorrah. This city had grown comfortable in a society that lived far from God, one that rejected His statutes, ordinances, and laws. The angels came to Lot and warned him and his family to "Get up!" and to "Run for your lives or you will be swept away! And do not look back!" In other words, do not turn away from your faith by turning back to your comforts and old ways. Do not become an example of the consequences of disobedience and worldliness.

We are called to be in this world, working for the good of the Kingdom of Heaven and for our neighbors, not to be contaminated by the rebellion of this world. This story also illustrates how distractions can hinder those seeking to follow Jesus. Not only did I look back—I ran to grab one last thing! I was trying to fit God into my life, taking Him out when I needed Him or when it seemed appropriate. But God is life: He is reality and should be in every part of our lives. I had it backward then; it's not a question of how to squeeze Him into our lives. The walk with God is not a hobby, it is a lifestyle. We also have free will to choose: God is not interested in prisoners. But understand that the choices we make matter. Be intentional in what you give your "yes" and attention to. God said to be in the world but not of the world. God created man, blessed him and said to subdue the earth. God created man in His image; that with Him we can conquer. God didn't plan for His children to be apart from Him in Spirit. With God, through the Holy Spirit, there is nothing you cannot do. That means to get up and remember your inheritance as God's children. He showed me that He is indeed all-knowing, knowing I was going to kick my feet and rant as I did when he already answered my question in a dream the night before.

This was another chapter in my life that was hard to write

and revisit. Clearly, I was young and immature—how embarrassing. And God does discipline those He loves so take heart in it. Not everything is from the enemy.

Hebrews 12:3–7
For consider him who endured such hostility from sinners against himself, so that you won't grow weary and give up. In struggling against sin, you have not yet resisted to the point of shedding your blood. And you have forgotten the exhortation that addresses you as sons: My son, do not take the Lord's discipline lightly or lose heart when you are reproved by him, for the Lord disciplines the one He loves and punishes every son He receives. Endure suffering as discipline: God is dealing with you as sons. For what son is there a father does not discipline?

Galatians 5:16–17
I say, then, walk by the Spirit and you will certainly not carry out the desire of the flesh. For the flesh desires what is against the Spirit, and the Spirit desires what is against the flesh; these are opposed to each other, so that you don't do what you want.

Deuteronomy 30:1–3
When all these things happen to you—the blessings and curses I have set before you—and you come to your senses while you are in all the nations where the Lord your God has driven you, and you and your children return to the Lord your God and obey him with all your heart and all your soul by

doing everything I am commanding you today, then he will restore your fortunes, have compassion on you, and gather you again from all the places where the LORD your God has scattered you.

1 Peter 5:10
The God of all grace, who called you to his eternal glory in Christ, will himself restore, establish, strengthen, and support you after you have suffered a little while.

Phew, I was struggling. God has brought me a long way. I remember these moments like they were yesterday, and I can truly say: God is so good. The woman He has built from the inside testifies to this—if you're going through this now, hear me: you have better and brighter days ahead. Keep going. Keep trusting. I know those words might sound just as frustrating and infuriating as they did for me back then, but I promise you that if you keep your focus on Him, you will come out stronger on the other side. One day you will look back and see how the enemy was working overtime to keep you stuck where you were, and sometimes that enemy can be your own stubbornness. Keep fighting.

The biggest mistake I was making was looking outside myself for the answer. Don't misunderstand me here—it is important to commune with the body of Christ, for iron sharpens iron. But nothing replaces a personal relationship with God. You must know His voice for yourself. And that does not come from someone else doing the work for you. I believe that's why so many miss out on truly experiencing God. It's not an easy walk. Like any relationship, it takes time, consistency, and intimacy. God said, "Seek me with all thy heart and I will answer you." That may sound simple and straightforward but getting your heart into the right posture is a process. There is a big difference between *looking* for God and *seeking* God with all your heart.

Matthew 6:33
"But seek first the kingdom of God and his righteousness, and all these things will be provided for you."

Jeremiah 29:10–14
"I will attend to you and will confirm my promise concerning you to restore you to this place. For I know the plans I have for you"—this is the LORD's *declaration—"plans for your well-being, not for disaster, to give you a future and hope. You will call to me and come and pray to me, and I will listen to you. You will seek me and find me when you search for me with all your heart. I will be found by you."*

THE ADVERSARY'S RECRUITING TACTICS

This day, I was exhausted. I hadn't slept much after morning prayer, and I rarely ever go back to bed—but this morning, I felt that my body needed rest. Before starting the day's Scripture, I grabbed some trash bags and cleaned house again. Anything questionable—anything that stirred doubt in my spirit—went straight into the bags. By the time I finished, I felt clearer.

Lighter. This day's reading was Psalm 35, and it hit me powerfully. As I read, it felt like prayer pouring straight from my spirit. I had a knowing in that moment: I need to pray more.

Later, I ran a few errands, and I took Sav with me. The fresh air felt good, like a small reset. While waiting over an hour for my groceries, I noticed something different about myself—I wasn't upset. I didn't phase me one bit. Normally, I would have been rushing, frustrated, ready to go. Instead, I was calm, patient, even peaceful. I liked this version of me.

While waiting, I started checking my personal emails for the day. The very first subject line that stood out read: "You are being fooled." I checked the sender—I had never received mail from this person or establishment before. In that moment, I had a knowing that it was spiritual. I remembered what the prayer instructor said just a few days earlier; "the enemy will always come back to try to deceive." I backed out of my inbox and went to organize my photos and videos.

The suggested presentation of files was named "Golden Hour." It began with a clip of me on the beach in Nantucket, then rolled into picture after picture of the ocean, the water, and the sun. Normally, people see the ocean and feel peace and beauty. But for me, during this season, the ocean was a reminder of my battle with marine spirits. It was like spiritual warfare disguised as nostalgia. I didn't give it any more thought; I closed it and moved on.

The next day, I was up at 5:30 a.m. for prayer. That morning, I started to use some of the time to pause and reflect—life was moving fast. I started with my life and marriage generally.

I made two lists: what makes me happy and what does not. By the time I finished, I had three pages filled. Some parts brought me to tears.

From there my day unraveled quickly into one challenge after another. The first blow was a notification that my student loan servicer had changed. This frustrated me because I had planned to pay off the balance the year before. But my husband suggested that I invest my money instead—said it would be the smarter move. I took his advice. And it was the better choice: I just didn't want to deal with the change, in this moment it didn't soften or help me having to deal with it while I had a busy schedule. I tried to get ahead of it so I wouldn't have to think about it again. I called the company to get clarity on the changes and every representative I reached seemed completely lost—misinformed and confused. At one point it seemed they were intentionally incompetent, or it was their first job ever. It felt like hours of wasted time, endless circles, and absolutely nothing accomplished. I couldn't get ahold of someone long enough to even just pay it off.

During this time, it had only been two days since my grandmother's passing. I was helping with funeral arrangements and preparing the obituary, which was due that evening. My plate was full, and while I normally work well under pressure, this felt different.

I sat at the kitchen island, trying to grab a quick bite between tasks. But in that moment, I didn't want to be strong anymore. I took a minute to be still. I rested my head in my arms, the same way we used to in grade school, when the teacher told us to put our heads down for quiet time. That was the last time I remember being in this position. But in this moment, it was exactly what I needed. I sat with myself in stillness.

When I lifted my head, a new email popped up in my inbox—a rejection from Microsoft. That one stung a bit. I was sure I had it in the bag. I was qualified, confident, and hopeful about making a move to that company. It took me by surprise. Now I'm thinking—I need Jesus. I opened my Bible to read Psalm 37. As I read, I cried. The words were exactly what I needed in that moment, but still, the weight of reality hadn't lifted. My situation hadn't changed, the tasks remained, and the grief was still heavy. I began having thoughts about all the people who read the same words for comfort in their time of despair. Clinging to them for relief. And I wondered—*When? When does all this truly happen? When does His promise break through?*

In this moment of questioning God's Word with tears in my eyes I looked up and another email had just come through. The subject read: "We can make it easier for you, Brittany." Again, I checked the sender. Again, it was from an establishment I had never received mail from before. And again, I knew instantly—it was spiritual. At that moment, I could see the enemy. He had made the wrong move. And my entire perspective changed in that very moment—he wasn't going to win. I raised my head and with all the authority in me declared aloud: *I serve one God and one God only. God Almighty: creator of all, in the mighty name of Jesus Christ.*

THE TRUTH I KNOW NOW

Learning to trust God is a process: it requires deep faith. On this walk, I've come to understand that rejection is often God's redirection, and trials are opportunities to build endurance. At this time in my life, I was still trying to plan and create my life, my way. I wasn't sure how to rest in Him and surrender to His way. This took time to unlearn. Surrendering that way of being, and truly learning to wait on God's way, took time. It required me to slow down, to listen, and to step through only the doors He opened.

Over the years, I've realized there are countless counterfeit doors: they're decorated nicely with the wreath of the season, shiny bells and whistles, and I've walked through many of them. Each one left me right back where I started—unfulfilled. These counterfeit doors are nothing more than well-dressed distractions—time stealers designed to keep you caught in cycles of chasing what doesn't matter. Far from your true purpose, the very life God has ordained for you. The truth I know now is this: praise Him in your storms just as your praise Him in your blessings. He is faithful in both.

James 1:2–8,12

Consider it a great joy, my brother and sisters, whenever you experience various trials, because you know that the testing of your faith produces endurance. And let endurance have its full effect, so that you may be mature and complete, lacking nothing. Now if any of you lacks wisdom, he should ask God—who gives to all generously and ungrudgingly—and it will be given to him. But let him ask in faith without doubting. For the doubter is like the surging sea, driven and tossed by the wind. That person should not expect to receive anything from the Lord, being double-minded and unstable in all his ways. Blessed is the one who endures trials, because when he has stood the test, he will receive the crown of life that God has promised to those who love him.

PART THREE

God's Grace

The Road to Restoration

I got into the mentorship. I joined without knowing what to expect, but I was excited. It was a seven-week commitment, and I had prepared myself for the journey. One of the weeks overlapped with a vacation we had already booked in Aruba. I hoped it wouldn't interfere, but either way, I was committed—wholeheartedly. Once the dates were confirmed, I began planning my fasting and meetings around the trip.

The group was small—seven of us, plus the mentorship instructor. It was an international gathering of extraordinary women, an experience I hold close to my heart, and I will never forget. I consider these women now family in Christ, and the mentorship itself as a critical stepping stone in my pursuit of God.

Before our first meeting, we received preparation material and assignments to complete. It felt like I was back in college, and it quickly became a full commitment—mentally, physically, and emotionally. By the time we entered the second week, I was in Aruba. That week, we were each assigned a prayer partner. The assignment was simple but profound: one week of dedicated prayer for your partner, focusing on what they needed most in their life. We also fasted to limit interference while communing with the Holy Spirit. My mind ran wild with doubts. I'm just a baby Christian, I thought. Everyone else seemed like seasoned veterans of faith. Meanwhile I was still learning the books of the Bible and trying to get familiar with them. While trying to keep up with this new jargon—words were flying around that

I never heard before—I thought, *What if I don't hear anything? What if I let my partner down?* Still, I stuck to the fast. I went into it with all my heart, gave it everything I had, and prayed for God to meet me.

My prayer partner's name was Ryan. She and I were the only two from the United States, which I thought was great from a time zone perspective. We connected right after the mentorship session. I remember receiving a text from her before I even had the chance to gather my thoughts. I smiled when I saw it and thought, *Yeah, I like her, she's on it.* But when I opened her message, it was written in Greek. Literally—Greek letters. It was so strange. I had been getting texts and calls with no problem. Coincidence? No, I knew it wasn't. I emailed her instead, and thankfully, we were able to communicate clearly, setting up our plan and call schedule for daily prayer share sessions each day.

It was a Monday, and I was sitting on the beach when I heard the words: "The long way home." I wasn't sure what it meant, so I sat in silence a little longer. Then I heard: "Book." At the time my focus was on my partner, so I pulled out my notebook and started writing what I was receiving. My first thought was, *Maybe she's an author and this is for her next book?* Then I heard "book" again. For four days, I received nothing—dry silence. I began to wonder, what if this doesn't mean anything to her? What if "the long way home" is just random? I'm going to sound crazy coming back with this.

Then on the fifth day, after praying for her, I saw a vision: the word "prudence" and the Scripture reference of Proverbs

8:32–36. Relief washed over me. I sat in awe at how beautiful it is to be fully dedicated to praying for someone else in God—someone who, at this point, was still a complete stranger. It was such a different kind of love and care than what the world teaches. That in itself was a lesson for me: even if I had received nothing at all, the act of interceding for another was already a gift.

It was challenging to be on vacation and deny myself all the things that people usually indulge in—eating, relaxing, staying up late, sleeping in, enjoying a margarita. I didn't expect my husband to join me on this journey, and trust me, he didn't volunteer either. But at this point in my life, nothing else mattered but seeking God with all my heart. I was focused on Him—locked in. That morning, my husband had planned an early hike. We had to be at the trail at 6:30 a.m., which I thought was perfect since I was fasting. Hiking early meant I'd avoid the worst of the heat. I was on a twelve-hour fast—no food and no water. The hardest part was resisting our morning tradition: stopping at our favorite coffee shop. The smell of fresh coffee hit me hard, but I chose to stay faithful to my walk and commitment to my partner.

When we met our guide, he explained the hike and did the usual health checks—one being the need to carry water. My husband quickly shared that I was fasting; it seemed he had been eagerly awaiting the opportunity to snitch. I assured the guide I'd be fine: I was in good hands. Along the trail, the guide stopped to show us a cactus, explaining that its berries could provide water in an emergency if one was ever in need while in the desert. He plucked one for himself, then handed some to us. I passed at first, thinking, *What if an animal peed on that cactus?* My husband tasted one, then passed one to me again and said, "It's really good, try it." Without hesitation, I did. Immediately I remembered: I was fasting. I voiced it out loud, out of shock that I forgot that quickly. My husband causally replied, "Oh yeah, I forgot." I looked at him and wondered if he had truly forgotten. I felt betrayed, like Adam in the Garden of Eden. I said a quick prayer in my heart and kept walking, realizing I could not lean on him—or anyone—for this journey. I had to remain present and alert. As we continued, I had a knowing: "Snake on the path." The guide led, I was in the middle, and my husband followed behind me. I asked the guide if there were snakes in the area. He shook his head confidently. "No, not here. We're on the west side of the island. The snakes are on the other side, many miles away." About ten minutes later, the guide suddenly froze. "Whoa, whoa, whoa—don't move." My body stiffened as my eyes scanned for danger. He slowly pointed downward—less than two feet from where my next step would have landed was a snake, its head coiled and waiting, perfectly camouflaged in the brush and shrubbery.

He, very cautiously and skillfully, picked up the snake and explained to us that he needed to go ahead of us and kill it, as it was dangerous—an invasive species on the island. He identified it as a boa constrictor: a non-native predator that threatened the island's ecosystem. My husband looked at me, and I at him—we both knew what had just happened. We continued on, keeping a safe distance behind our guide. That vacation time was a challenge. I realized that when you consciously take a stand for God and commit to walking the narrow path, the illusions around you start to reveal themselves—some subtle, others boldly in your face. One night, while walking the boardwalk after dinner, we came across a popular beach bar on the water. They had live music, with songs played by request. My husband wanted to check it out and stop for a beer. I don't drink beer, and on this trip, I had given up alcohol altogether. I compromised. This was *my* walk, not his, and I didn't expect him to understand—or force him to join me. I whispered a prayer, and we headed down the dock. The vibe was nice, he had a few beers, and I had an iced tea. We enjoyed the music—lots of old school classics, with a relaxed, lively vibe. Watching people drink while staying sober was an entirely different experience: both entertaining and eye-opening. As I sat there, I silently prayed: Lord, *how is all this going to work?* But as the sound of music filled the air, I froze: "*When you walk through a storm, hold your head up high and don't be afraid of the dark ... Walk on through the wind, walk on through the rain ... Though your dreams be tossed and blown ... walk on, walk on, with hope in your heart, and you'll never walk alone.*"

I couldn't believe what I was hearing. I was stunned. Was this a song about God blazing through the speakers at 9 p.m. at a beach bar in Aruba? It most certainly was. I never heard that song before, and never would I have expected to hear it in a setting like that. The artist's name is Andrea Bocelli. Honestly, it's not a song I would have ever chosen for myself, but now it holds a special place in my heart as a reminder of God's omnipresence and tender attention. I was blown away and again sat in awe, with a smile and laugh of joy.

Psalms 139:7–12
Where can I go to escape your Spirit? Where can I flee from your presence. If I go up to heaven, you are there, if I make my bed in Sheol, you are there. If I fly on the wings of the dawn and settle down on the western horizon even there you will lead me. If I say, "Surely the darkness will hide me, and the light around me will be night—even the darkness is not dark to you. The night shines like the day; darkness and light are alike to you."

I had made it through vacation. Once we were back home, life began to settle into its usual rhythm. I had a call scheduled with my partner to share what I had received during prayer over the seven-day period before our next group mentorship call. I was excited—and a little nervous—hoping that what I had received would help and encourage her in her walk.

What I received for Ryan:

- "*The Long Way Home*," "book"
- Confidence and protection
- The word "prudence" and Proverbs 8:32–36: "And now, sons, listen to me; those who keep my ways are happy. Listen to instruction and be wise; don't ignore it. Anyone who listens to me is happy, watching at my doors every day, waiting by the posts of my doorway.

For the one who finds me finds life and obtains favor from the LORD, but the one who misses me harms himself; all who hate me love death."

What Ryan received for me:

- Psalm 46:5: "God is in the midst of her; she shall not be moved. God shall help her, and that right early."
- "Esther," "He is going to give you favor with your king."
- "Book"

We shared what we received for one another with much joy, love, and laughter. She told me that she'd been praying for wisdom and favor for months. I told her about the Andrea Bocelli song at the beach bar. And together we both came to realize something remarkable: The "book" we had both heard about was mine. That author had been me. These are moments of my life I will forever cherish.

Let Your Light Shine

When I woke up this morning, I had been reminded of this dream while reading my Dad's morning Scripture share.

Dad's Daily Scripture

Morning family, you know what time it is. Today's bible verse comes from the book of Matthew 5:16; vs16-Let your light so shine before men, that they may see your good works, and glorify your father which is in heaven. Amen. Let us seek to grow through humble obedience to His Word so that our life may grow in grace and in a knowledge of the Lord Jesus Christ. Let us walk in the spirit maturing in Christ, so we may be filled to the measure of all the fullness of God, according to His power that is at work within us. Let us remember these words that Matthew wrote, and as the days get darker, let us shine the light of Jesus into a world that desperately needs His life-giving, light of Life. Amen. Until tomorrow, have a bless day, and always keep the faith and our LORD God will always keep you. Amen.

"Let your light shine before men": this brought me back to the dream I had the night before.

Dream: Let Your Light Shine Before Men

I was walking in what felt like a covered parking garage and was heading to travel somewhere by train. As I was walking to the station, I saw a strange man. He came up to me and quickly reached for the door to the station and opened it for me. This transportation place was fancy, I remember the door and everything on the inside looked soft and plush. When he opened the door, he said what sounded like "all praise to Yahweh," softly. I asked, "did you say Yahweh?"; he answered, "yes." I replied with a smile as I walked through the door.

When we made it inside the station, he started to speak to me prophetically, it was like he was not human. He said, *"look at you, like royalty and you shine like glitter." "You walk with many, I see, Yoruba."* He also said another name that I couldn't recall when I woke. I replied, *"but Yoruba practices serve many different Orishas"* and I asked him *"what do you mean by this? I only serve YHWH the one and only."* He said *"yes, but many gods are after you, coming over and above you: they want you."* I asked, *"what do I do"* and his response I could not recall after waking.

End of Dream

This man was shapeshifting. When he opened the door, hooded, he appeared to be an African man, but when I got a better look at him while we talked face to face, I realized I could not place a nationality to him—he looked majestic. Yet, I knew this man. I knew his spirit. The things he spoke drew me back to a divination I had years earlier with an African spiritualist. It took me back specifically to what that spiritualist told me during the divination:

- "This is big: it's better to walk into this consciously than unconsciously."
- "You are regal."
- "Your light is so bright so powerful; it is not subject to further dissection or understanding it is taken as is."

That man, too, had the ability to shapeshift. The words "regal" and "royalty" were something I was told many times in divinations from different people. One tarot reader even twisted the narrative, telling me a story about how I supposedly came from a royal line in Egypt.

THE TRUTH I KNOW NOW

It is no light of my own, but the marvelous light of the LORD. I am a people of His possession so that I may proclaim the praises of the one who called me out of the darkness into His marvelous light. I was blessed to see this Scripture play out in dream just the night before my Dad shared it. In the dream, the man recognized the light within me and glorified our Father in heaven. God does not give us gifts to hide, nor a light to place under the table. Let your light shine and represent the Kingdom of God.

1 Peter 2:9
But you are a chosen race, a royal priesthood, a holy nation, a people for His possession so that you may

proclaim the praises of the one who called you out of darkness into his marvelous light.

Matthew 5:12–16 (KJV)

"Rejoice and be exceedingly glad, for great is your reward in heaven, for so they persecuted the prophets who were before you. You are the salt of the earth; but if the salt loses its flavor, how shall it be seasoned? It is then good for nothing but to be thrown out and trampled underfoot by men. You are the light of the world. A city that is set on a hill cannot be hidden. Nor do they light a lamp and put it under a basket, but on a lampstand, and it gives light to all who are in the house. Let your light shine before men, that they may see your good works and glorify your Father in heaven."

Trusting God

The walk with Jesus is not always sunshine and butterflies—you have to put in the work. I remember many hard nights, battling so much in the spirit—so much spiritual warfare. But the truth I know now is this: the enemy doesn't fight people who aren't a threat, and God doesn't give you battles that you aren't equipped to fight. On this particular day, I felt defeated and was in my thoughts. I was disappointed in many things, the biggest being the choices I had made for my life up to that point. I opened my study Bible to insert chapter tabs and landed on a page with an excerpt titled "When You Feel Stuck." God is so great.

This passage spoke to Joseph's life, illustrating how setbacks can be divine detours. God gave him dreams of rising to power, and when he shared them with his brothers, their jealousy led them to betray him. Sold into slavery and later falsely accused, Joseph endured years of hardship before God elevated him to power in Egypt. Those trials prepared him for his destiny and set the stage for his leadership. Looking back, Joseph recognized God's greater plan, telling his brothers, "You planned evil against me; God planned it for good."

Sometimes what you're going through may not make sense, it may hurt and seem unfair. But remember, lean not on your own understanding for His thoughts are not our thoughts and His ways are not our ways. The very things I thought broke me back then, I now see were working for my good. Trust God's detours—He uses them to lead you to your purpose. As the *Tony Evans Study Bible* states (p. 63): "The life of Joseph provides a perfect example of how life's disappointments can actually be detours in disguise. Do not lose heart; God hasn't forgotten about you. He's just not taking you to your destiny in a straight line. Trust the detours God brings your way. He uses them to take you from where you are to where He wants you to be."

2 Timothy 4:16–18

At my first defense, no one stood by me, but everyone deserted me. May it not be counted against them. But the LORD stood with me and strengthened me, so that I might fully preach the word, and all the Gentiles might hear it. I was rescued from the lion's mouth. The LORD will rescue me from every evil work and will bring me safely into his heavenly kingdom. To Him be the glory forever and ever! Amen.

Mark 6:4

Jesus said to them, "A prophet is not without honor except in his hometown, among his relatives, and in his household."

Genesis 50:20

"You planned evil against me; God planned it for good to bring about the present result: the survival of many people."

THE DOUBLE MINDED: TRUST HIS TIMING

There will be seasons of discomfort. This day I was struggling. I prayed in the car with tears in my eyes asking God to restore me, to allow me to feel joy again—I no longer felt alive. I was drained by the people around me. I prayed for Him to help me trust Him. I had no idea how this would work; for so long, I had relied on what I believed was my own strength—me making it happen, me doing the work. I was learning what a real relationship with God looked and felt like, not with some parts of my life but all. I was learning how to truly be one with Him, how to be aligned and in position.

THE TRUTH I KNOW NOW

I was afraid to trust His timing. Back then, I trusted Him only with pieces of my life. The truth is: it was never by my strength or by my might but by His Spirit. I was lukewarm.

1 Kings 18:21
Then Elijah approached all the people and said, "How long will you waver between two opinions? If the LORD is God, follow Him. But if Baal, follow him."

Zechariah 4:6
"Not by strength or by might, but by my Spirit," says the LORD of Armies.

I was, at this point, trying to rely on Him one hundred percent. Some days I felt steady and I fully trusted that He would see me through, and other days I was terrified. Documenting everything was very time consuming, but I held onto the knowing I had received long ago: "Everything will matter." "Everything will make sense." The LORD's work is never done in vain—so I continued. This day, as I journaled, the Holy Spirit gave me a word:

Revelation 3:15–17
"I know your works, that you are neither cold nor hot. I wish that you were cold or hot. So then, because you are lukewarm, and neither hot nor cold, I am about to spit you out of my mouth. For you say, 'I'm rich; I have become wealthy and need nothing,' and you don't realize that you are wretched, miserable, poor, blind, and naked."

I drove to my destination with this heavy on my heart. I wasn't sure what to do with it. I didn't want to be spat out, but I also didn't know how to fully surrender and stop trying to control what I thought was best for my life. Before getting out of the car, I opened an image-sharing app—and without scrolling, a message appeared front and center:

"The devil tries to get you to worry about the future so you can't focus on the joy in your life right now. Enjoy every minute, because life is a gift from God. Joel 2:25: 'I will restore to you years that the swarming locusts have eaten.'"

I sat with this for a moment, receiving it with tears in my eyes. I realized I had to get out of my own way. When I got back home, I looked up Joel to read the full Scripture. Before I even finished, I fell to my knees in prayer and thanksgiving.

Joel 2:23–27

Children of Zion, rejoice and be glad in the LORD your God, because he gives you the autumn rain for your vindication. He sends showers for you, both autumn and spring rain as before. The threshing floors will be full of grain and the vats will overflow with new wine and fresh oil. I will repay you for the years the locusts have eaten—the great locust and the young locust, the other locusts and the locust swarm—my great army that I sent among you. You will have plenty to eat and be satisfied. You will praise the name of the LORD your God, who has dealt wondrously with you. My people will never again be put to shame. You will know that I am present and that I am the LORD your God, and there is no other. My people will never again be put to shame.

1 Corinthians 15:58

Therefore, my dear brothers and sisters, be steadfast, immovable, always excelling in the LORD's work, because you know that your labor in the LORD is not in vain.

THE TRUTH I KNOW NOW

Trust Him—you're not in control anyway.

James 1:5–8

Now if any of you lacks wisdom, he should ask God—who gives to all generously and ungrudgingly—and it will be given to him. But let him ask in faith without

> doubting. For the doubter is like the surging sea, driven and tossed by the wind. That person should not expect to receive anything from the LORD, being double-minded and unstable in all his ways.

Later that evening, I called my parents for our Bible study. It had all started when I shared a message with them one day about the LORD, and from that moment, our study time was born. It flowed naturally, and we've continued ever since. When I first called the house, no one answered, so I tried my Mom's cell. She was out with a friend and on her way back, and said she'd call as soon as she got home.

By then, it was late, and I was exhausted from the day. I was ready to settle into bed early and felt that I should just text her and suggest we skip study for the night and pick it back up tomorrow. But just as I reached for my phone, I saw a missed call from her only minutes earlier. When I called her back, her first words were, "Okay, you ready?" How could I say no to that? I went up to my office and got ready for study. At the end, I shared my daily devotional reading with them since I hadn't gotten to it yet. As I read it aloud, I held back tears: God is so good.

New Things
(Sara Perry, *365 Days of Courage*, p. 27)

Behold, the former things have come to pass, Now I declare new things; Before they sprout, I proclaim them to you" (Isaiah 42:9). In the changing seasons, we catch glimpses of the old things passing away. We create space in the simplicity of winter to let go of what we need to clear away in our lives as we prepare for the barren months. We anticipate new life come spring. The rhythms of nature are cyclical, as are the rhythms of our lives. We do not stay in endless summer with long days in the sun and bounty surrounding us, nor do we dwell forever in a never-ending winter. May we garner hope from the changes of the seasons, remembering God's Word and his promises as we do so. Even before new life sprouts, God gives us glimpses of it. He shares with us ever so graciously, the hope we need in the waiting.

Back to Bible Study

After we closed our Bible study session, I planned to do a bit more reading. I went back to Isaiah 42:9 to read the full Scripture for context, but when I reached the chapter I noticed that verses 5–9 were already highlighted. I paused, wondering, *When did I read this?* Maybe during one of the mentorship studies or prayer sessions? I wasn't sure. But as I sat with the words, tears filled my eyes. I had been in deep prayer about my purpose—about what all this meant and what exactly I was being called to do. And here was the Holy Spirit, reminding me that He had already planted the answer in His Word.

Isaiah 42:5–9

This is what God, the LORD, says—who created the heavens and stretched them out, who spread out the earth and what comes from it, who gives breath to the people on it and spirit *to those who walk on it—"I am the L*ORD*. I have called you for a righteous purpose, and I will hold you by your hand, I will watch over you, and I will appoint you to be a covenant for the people and a light to the nations, in order to open blind eyes, to bring out prisoners from the dungeon, and those sitting in darkness from the prison house. I am the L*ORD*, that is my name, and I will not give my glory to another or my praise to idols. The past events have indeed happened. Now I declare new events, I announce them to you before they occur."*

THE TRUTH I KNOW NOW

Being a "doer," it was hard to place my destiny in the hands of something I could not see. I now understand that this is the true meaning of faith. For all my fellow challenge seekers—give this one a go. It was, and continues to be, the most challenging and most rewarding thing I've ever done on every level. The truth is, we are not really in control as much as we like to believe anyway—so just let it go, and let God.

Hebrews 11:1
Now faith is the reality of what is hoped for, the proof of what is not seen.

Zechariah 4:6
"Not by strength or by might, but by my Spirit," says the LORD of Armies.

Trusting God

During this time of my life, as I was 'running back' to God. I dedicated my entire being to Him. I was seeking Him. I made fasting a part of my lifestyle, rose for 4 a.m. prayer, and I lived on the Word: God was my bread and butter. On this morning, I was up for 4 a.m. prayer. When I got to my prayer room, I heard, as a knowing, *"You left your phone downstairs, and she is going to call today."* I thought maybe it's just wishful thinking. I had always welcomed my parents to join me for morning prayer and fasting when seeking God. I know that 4 a.m. prayer isn't for everyone—it's a hard sell—but when you are seeking God, you look forward to that quiet time with the Father, whenever you can get it. I continued to my prayer room to get started. I had a dream I needed to take into prayer for clarity: I wrote it down and then went into prayer.

When I finished, I went back downstairs to get my phone. I had three missed calls from my Mom. I called her back, hoping she hadn't dozed off in the time it took me to return the call. Just then I heard her voice: *"Hello, I'm sorry if I woke you. Were you up?"* If you could see how big my smile was in that moment. I headed back to my prayer room, and as we were getting ready to pray again, she said, *"Hold on one minute, your Dad just got up and said wait for him."* My heart was so full in this moment—I couldn't hold back my tears; they were tears of joy, giving all the glory and praise to the LORD. Our God is a living God, and He endures forever.

The Call Is Not Always Comfortable

On this day, my parents and I began the Book of Ezekiel for Bible study. I wasn't sure why, but it was what I heard in my spirit. My parents asked why Ezekiel, and the only answer I could give was that it was where we were supposed to be. Before we got started, my Mom told us that she had something she wanted to share with the group before we began. She said she had prayed and asked God if there was a book He wanted her to read. She felt led to Genesis and, within that book, she landed on this excerpt from the study Bible commentary (*Tony Evans Study Bible*, p. 6):

> Will God be "Lord God" to you? Or will you just say that he is "God" while making your own decisions? Whenever you allow the evil one to cause you to question the ultimate authority of God in your life, you jeopardize your influence in God's kingdom. That is why so many Christians never fully live out their destinies.

What a revelation it was indeed for my Mom. I pressed a bit—I had to—so will He? With love and gentleness, we laughed. But God will correct; He will highlight the parts of us that need attention, and He will reveal them. The question is: Are you listening, and are you willing?

God's word is living, and He is good. I shared how important it is not to forget or take these moments for granted. What a beautiful and convicting revelation it was. And with that we moved into our study of Ezekiel.

This weekend we were staying at my fathers-in-law's to help with day-to-day tasks around the house and care for him after his surgery. This was one part of my life where I had to lie in the bed I made. Being unequally yoked in marriage when it comes to faith brings its own assortment of spiritual battles. I kept in step with the Holy Spirit and remained steadfast on my walk. I prepared the studies for the time I would be there and informed my parents I would be there for a couple days and we would continue to study at the same time.

The first morning waking there, I rose with a heaviness and sadness. I asked God for strength. In that moment, I realized that the closer I drew near to God, the more I became aware of how far I had strayed in so many areas of my life—how many decisions I had made without Him for my life. I knew I was reaping what I had sown: sleeping in the bed I had made. The price you pay when you make your own choices apart from the LORD is often the harder walk, because His will will always be done. Like Jonah, you can choose the hard way or the easier way. That morning, I reflected on the importance of shared faith in marriage. Spiritually, there is an agreement that takes place when two people come together—it's far more than just the physical. I didn't yet have a relationship with God then, I just knew my husband was a good man.

I heard my father-in-law getting up, preparing to do puja, as he normally does. By this point, he knew my stance regarding my faith and worship to God Almighty alone. Last week, my husband and I had been there helping, and during that visit I had made my beliefs clear. While I was in deep conversation with my husband, my father-in-law came over to bless me with his hands over my head. I quickly moved aside and said, *"oh no, no thank you. I only serve one God."* I then continued my conversation, feeling stern and realizing afterward that I could have been gentler or even shared more about Jesus in that moment. I was caught off guard, and he was simply doing what he normally does.

This morning, I stayed in the bedroom a bit longer reading and holding on to my peace. Moments later, he came into the bedroom with his hands cupped from puja, in hopes that this time I would take the blessings. I reminded him respectfully that I cannot accept his blessing.

> He said, *"I can't believe you reject my blessing. You know these are blessings from his mother and family."*
>
> I replied by correcting what I was rejecting that which is not true. I replied, *"you pray to many deities as well. I can't accept those blessings. I pray and serve one God through our Lord and Savior Jesus Christ."*
>
> He replied: *"I have Jesus Christ up there too."*
>
> My reply: *"You should not. He doesn't not belong there: that is blasphemy."*
>
> He replied: *"Yes, one God but these others (deities) are just prayers help in going to Him."*

I replied: *"God says serve no other gods and put no other gods before Him."*

He walked out of the room, saying: *"No, no, that is not true."*

As you can imagine, this is not a simple conversation and by no means is it comfortable. It is sensitive and it's a discussion no one wants to have in this situation—but it is necessary when it comes to standing firm in your faith. My approach and intention were never to proselytize; I do not aim to change someone's beliefs, nor would I ever judge another's walk. The battle is not mine; it is the Lord's. He will do it. I respect that people have different views and beliefs. I am not here to convince or prove to anyone who God is, but I will remain obedient to Him in my walk.

I went to grab my Bible, and I shared the Word with him:

Exodus 20:1–6

Then God spoke all these words: "I am the Lord your God, who brought you out of the land of Egypt, out of the place of slavery. Do not have other gods besides me. Do not make an idol for yourself, whether in the shape of anything in the heavens above or on the earth below or in the waters under the earth. Do not bow in worship to them; for I, the Lord your God, am a jealous God, bringing the consequences of the father's iniquity on the children to the third and fourth generations of those who hate me, but showing faithful love to a thousand generations of those who love me and keep my commands."

He went on to question the authenticity of the Bible—its human authors, the time in which it was written, and so on. I knew where this conversation was going—I kept my composure. In that moment, I silently wondered, *Why dear Lord, why must I do this?* A call came through that he took in that moment. I walked out of the room and told him I would be nearby if he wanted to finish the conversation.

I prayed, questioning: *Why, why must I be here doing this. How would this ever work.* I accepted that I put myself in this position. But in this moment, I thought about the spiritual price I paid. I wept silently in prayer, pouring out my heart to the Lord.

THE TRUTH I KNOW NOW

Just how quickly I had forgotten what my Mom had shared yesterday before our Bible study (*Tony Evans Study Bible*, p. 6):

Will God be "Lord God" to you? Or will you just say that he is "God" while making your own decisions? Whenever you allow the evil one to cause you to question the ultimate authority of God in your life, you jeopardize your influence in God's kingdom. That is why so many Christians never fully live out their destinies.

Romans 8:28
We know that all things work together for the good of those who love God, who are called according to his purpose.

God may not always pull us out of a difficult situation right away. He may allow us to remain in it for a time, but He undoubtedly protects us while we're in it. Trust His plan and stay in step with the Holy Spirit. I was again reminded of who God is—and who are we to question how and why He uses us to reach and teach His children, especially when it's uncomfortable in the moment. Perhaps I am exactly where God intended for me to be.

Jesus did not come to bring peace and conform to the ways of the world or of people. This is a common misconception today, and it is painful to hear. This is war. As God's children, we are not called to live in comfort and complacency; we are called to be true representations of His Kingdom.

Matthew 10:34-36
"Don't assume that I came to bring peace on the earth. I did not come to bring peace, but a sword [Scripture]. For I came to turn a man against his father, a daughter against her mother, a daughter-in-law against her mother-in-law; and a man's enemies will be the members of his household."

I made it through the weekend, and once we returned home and settled in, I prepared for our Bible study. To my surprise God met me right there with an answered prayer. What a powerful revelation it was. We were on Ezekiel 2, and I froze in awe.

Ezekiel 2:4–7
The descendants are obstinate and hardhearted. I am sending you to them, and you must say to them, "This is what the

Lord God says." Whether they listen or refuse to listen—for they are a rebellious house—they will know that a prophet has been among them. But you, son of man, do not be afraid of them and do not be afraid of their words, even though briers and thorns are beside you and you live among scorpions. Don't be afraid of their words or discouraged by the look on their faces, for they are a rebellious house. Speak my words to them whether they listen or refuse to listen, for they are rebellious.

My God. He is so good, and He reigns supreme. I gave Him a renewed "yes" and surrender that night. The Holy Spirit revealed why we were in the Book of Ezekiel. Ultimately, Ezekiel teaches that God's greatest purpose is His glorification, and when we trust Him—even in rebellious or challenging circumstances—His plan prevails. When we live for His Kingdom, His presence becomes real to us and the world. Ezekiel was sent to give a message to the people in that the judgment they were experiencing was the result of their own sin. And I'm sure that was something they too did not want to hear. This book reminds us to seek out the Lord. It also gives us the opportunity to examine our lives and to make sure we are in alignment with God Almighty.

The Season of Building

I am entering my season of restoration. Sometimes God will break you down in order to build you back up in Him, this time on a solid foundation—on good soil. Up until this point, I had been sowing on rocky ground. I was building quickly, moving swiftly and creating the things I believed were good for me. But I had forgotten my roots—the very thing that holds you steady and nourishes you through a lifetime. Our God, the most important ingredient, knows what's best for you. His path and plans for your life are far greater than anything you could ever imagine for yourself. I gave Him my "yes," and it's the best decision I've ever made. Trust Him.

Matthew 13:5–6,8–9
"Other seed fell on rocky ground where it didn't have much soil, and it grew up quickly since the soil wasn't deep. But when the sun came up, it was scorched, and since it had no root, it withered away. Still other seed fell on good ground and produced fruit: some a hundred, some sixty, and some thirty times what was sown. Let anyone who has ears listen."

Proverbs 24:1–6
Don't envy the evil or desire to be with them, for their hearts plan violence, and their words stir up trouble. A house is built by wisdom, and it is established by understanding; by knowledge the rooms are filled with every precious and

beautiful treasure. A wise warrior is better than a strong one, and a man of knowledge than one of strength; for you should wage war with sound guidance—victory comes with many counselors.

THE BODY OF CHRIST

To God's people who were spiritual vessels, helpers, and sources of inspiration while I was in my valleys: thank you. We often have no idea how far our reach can be. Keep trusting God and allowing Him to lead you. If you have ever questioned—even for a moment—why you do what you do, let this be a testament for you.

For whoever needs the reminder, may this be one: *keep going!* Your calling and your work in the Kingdom are needed. Your assignment carries purpose. Many of the people who have helped me along this journey I do not know personally, some I have never met formally. Yet their obedience to the call and to the assignments God entrusted to them left a mark on my life—on the days I needed a word of encouragement or simply someone who truly believed and walked the narrow path.

The way back was not easy, and it was not quick: it was a process. There were moments when shame tried to silence me, when the weight of my past threatened to pull me under. But step by step, God showed me that His grace was greater than my guilt, His truth stronger than every lie I had once entertained.

I once thought my wandering had sealed my fate. Now I see that even my detours became part of His story—woven into a testimony of mercy, redemption, and love that never lets go. The chains I carried are broken. The road that once led me astray has become the very path that carried me home.

This is my story, but it is not mine alone. If you've ever felt lost, sitting in the wreckage of choices you never thought you'd make, or that you are too far gone, I want you to know this: our heavenly Father has not stopped waiting for you. He has not stopped loving you and His arms are open. His light still shines, and home is closer than you think.

Never underestimate the reach and power of the work you do for the Kingdom of God: it is truly immeasurable. The LORD's work is never done in vain. It's not an easy walk for those who truly commit to the way of Jesus Christ. May God continue to bless you, and may you remain steadfast in your faith. And may you be bold and courageous in your walk as we advance God's Kingdom agenda.

KEEP IN STEP WITH THE HOLY SPIRIT

This journey, and the many experiences I have been through, was one of the deepest, darkest valleys I have ever walked. Yet through it all, I emerged with an unshakable faith, love, and reverence for God Almighty and our Lord and Savior, Jesus Christ.

The journey was necessary.

One quote has stayed with me from that season, spoken by a mighty warrior in the Kingdom of God. These words aren't new—they've been echoed by many of the greats, but I can't tell you how many times they lifted me up when I didn't have spiritual support. One of her many sayings that still resonates with me is this:

> "God doesn't care about your accolades or your achievements. He created you; he knows how talented and special you are. He cares about who you become."
> —Latoya Okeia

In a world where you literally can become anything—and I mean *anything*—it is imperative that we keep our Creator in the details. He will not lead you astray. The world and its social conditioning aren't improving. We have, as a people, strayed far from truth and authenticity. Many people do not realize just how far they have drifted from their Creator until they are faced with tragedy.

Guard your heart and mind.

God is transcendent and immanent. Yet today, He is often treated as an afterthought. People have become deeply self-absorbed, focused on what they can gain or consume—in most cases on unprecedented levels—and yet it is never enough. Why? Because only God can fill that void. Save your money. If there was one thing I wish I had done differently in my life, it would be that I cultivated a relationship with God much sooner. This is very cliché, I know. But when I shared this sentiment with one of my close childhood friends, his response resonated deeply. I told him how I remembered his season seeking God in our early twenties, and how, where I am now in Christ, I recognize and admire the strength he showed during that time. He studied faithfully and fervently when I was living out my own will and my own life. I had an opportunity then, and just for a moment, I wondered how differently my life would have been had I joined him. He replied to my rambling by simply saying, "God knows his children and your time is now." I sat with that for a minute and thought, *Yes—perhaps you're right.*

Colossians 2:8–10
Be careful that no one takes you captive through philosophy and empty deceit based on human tradition, based on the elements of the world, rather than Christ. For the entire fullness of God's nature dwells bodily in Christ, and you have been filled by him, who is the head over every ruler and authority.

Revelation 3:11
"I am coming soon. Hold on to what you have, so that no one takes your crown."

Seek first the Kingdom of God and all else shall be established unto you. May God refresh and renew whatever has become stagnant in your life. May you not become weary in well doing: keep fighting the good fight and walking on the narrow path. I pray you remain steadfast in your faith. May God bless you and keep you always.

> "The greatest trick the devil ever pulled was convincing the world he didn't exist."
> —Charles Baudelaire

Epilogue: To the One Still Wandering

My story and journey are still being walked in faith, but I can say some of my most challenging days are behind me—all glory be to God. There is a refinement that takes place in the fire; you are not alone. Allow that fire to ignite the anointing of God upon your life. That same fire introduced me to the best version of myself. Thank God for the afflictions, the trials, tribulations, heartbreak, deceit and everything else that has tried to break you—for they will birth a version of you that you won't want to miss. Keep going. Keep fighting. He is with you, building you from the inside out. Do worry about what it looks like—just keep going!

Remember to whom you belong; you are more than a conqueror.

www.ingramcontent.com/pod-product-compliance
Lightning Source LLC
LaVergne TN
LVHW010313070526
83819LV00065B/5550